Memoirs of a Sales

Memoirs of a Sales Warrior: Part I
"My Life"

Ground Rules

Yes, this is not a "normal" book, so there are some things I hope you will do while reading.

Since chapters historically start on right side pages, there is often space left over on the preceding page. These are usually left blank, but not here. On every left side page that is not filled by an article, there will either be a page for notes, for you to jot down ideas, or what you have to do tomorrow, or a page for you to complete a task.

This book is designed to help you think and act. You might as well start right away.

Thanks again for reading my work.

Memoirs of a Sales Warrior: My Life, My Way

1ST printing: September 2002
2ND printing: February 2003

ISBN: 0972607404

Ideal Jacobs Corporation
515 Valley Street
Maplewood, NJ 07040
973-275-5100
fax 973-275-5161
www.idealjacobs.com
email: acj@idealjacobs.com

Published 2002, 2003 by Ideal Jacobs Corporation

Acknowledgements

The first time I spoke with Milvia DeZuani after she started to proofread this book, she had one question for me. "Are you as sure about life as you write?" she asked. My immediate answer was "Yes, I am sure". How can I know what it takes to sell, how do I know what will happen? History and experience is everything especially when dealing with the uncertainties of life and how people will react in given situations. Obviously I can't predict what will occur every time. However, over specific periods of time, under certain situations and on a percentage basis, I can be sure of some things.

If you try your hardest, have a modicum of intelligence and common sense, are honest, trustworthy and love what you do then I can predict with some certainty that you will be successful in whatever field you choose. The level of that success is based on your blend of personal talents, the area of business you are in and the climate of the times. It is not a question of whether you will succeed, but just by how much, and that rate again, is squarely in your hands.

It is very comforting to know that certain things "work." It is also very unsettling to realize that it does not matter so much what the world does because your destiny and rate of success are up to you, no excuses allowed. In the end, it is all your responsibility. You are the one that is accountable for the good and the bad. It is your effort that will define what happens.

It also helps if you can surround yourself with great people, which I have been incredibly fortunate in doing. I would like to thank Alice Prager, my second in command at Ideal Jacobs Corporation, who has been instrumental in the continuing and growing success of our company in general and my personal career in all areas in particular.

Our "MAC" computer guys David Creighton, Marc Appezzato and Mike Valentine who helped design, edit (sorry about my illegible handwritten changes) and prep this book to get ready for press.

I would also like to thank everyone at our company Ideal Jacobs for their support in general. You are all wonderful and it is an honor and privilege to be part of the same team.

To my three children Kayla, Alex and Ben I know I probably say this too much, but I think you are all wonderful, bright, creative great kids and it gives me unending joy to not only be your dad but to brag about you everywhere. I am proud of all of you!

And finally, thank you to my wife Wendy who has put up with all the phone calls, meetings, interrupted vacations and everything else associated with being married to someone who owns and runs a business. She has incredible patience and love for me that is boundless and has created a "home base" that has allowed me to soar to heights that would never have been possible without her.

INTRODUCTION

I love my job and my life, so it is now payback time.

I have always heard that there are no "rules" to life, no overall plan and everyone has to go day by day because no one knows what is going to happen.

I have been successfully selling for over twenty-five years and it has been my experience that there are "rules" which have been proven, over time, to predict what people will do, what things will happen and who will "win" when the game is over. If you know them then it makes it much easier to play and win to the extent, that you deserve, from your efforts, intelligence, determination and how much you want to win. My payback to you is telling you how the "game" of life works from my experience and how you can use it to your best advantage over time.

First let's define selling:

Selling is the exchange of goods or services between two people.

In order for the maximum amount of gain to be attained by all parties someone has to "know the rules." This book will give you my rules, plus a plethora of examples in the form of stories relating to them and my life.

Since you can't help being involved in selling (life) situations, you might as well become as good at them as possible. After all to maximize your own capabilities you need to be able to bring out the best in others.

Although there are 6 basic rules to selling there is no law that says you can't have fun while learning them. I love to laugh, learn, work and make money. Attaining your dreams does not necessarily mean enduring large amounts of drudgery, hardship and pain, it does mean a continual striving to improve yourself in all areas. This process often necessitates taking on new knowledge, accepting different ideas and learning about yourself. It also means being open to the opposite of what you thought before and being able to accept information in the way it is presented as opposed to the way you wish it was given. Therefore, do not expect an easy time.

But I am getting ahead of myself, my world is about to open up to you, use it for all it is worth, increase your happiness, make more money, love more people and spread it around. When it comes down to it, the most fun in life we have is when we are helping others, because it is the result of that often brings us our greatest success.

A few random thoughts...

by Jim Jensen

I have been fortunate in my life. In actuality, my existence has been blessed. My fortunes and travails have both been challenging and reward filled. As I told the beautiful woman, who was later to become my second wife "...stick with me as I am the luckiest man in the world."

I bring this to mind, just completed reading the newest book written by Andrew Jacobs. I have known Andy for twenty years now and consider his acquaintance one of the great joys in my life.

My first meeting, Andrew had a position as a salesman for a second generation company working for his father. That alone carried my respect as I had failed in being successful in a venture with my own father. We had been too similar and opinionated to make it work. Somehow, despite the similarities of Andrew to his father (which he still denies), he was able to subordinate his ego for his own best interest. Week after week, Andrew called upon me to purchase services from his printing company. It was probably eighteen months later when, I gave Ideal-Jacobs the only business that I have ever subscribed to them.

Long before that time, I was hooked. I am not sure what the attraction between us was at the time and only in retrospect am able to identify some of those factors.

As for my part, raised in a family of successful salesman, I recognized the initiative, drive, and absolute commitment to success that Andrew showed and was immediately grateful for his attitude to excel. In business, he, like the finest waiter in the best restaurant, mysteriously appeared with the answer at the most opportune time and, as quickly, disappeared.

Andrew was also an athlete, a very talented tennis player. The competitive drive that permeated this excellence was not lost as he crossed the base line into his other lives. In short, he was the challenge that I needed.

I have easily dispatched the pretenders. I would just finesse them to an area where I had expertise or, even better, analyze their weakness in their chosen arena, work harder and beat them on their own court. My fascination with Andrew... he does the same.

My life with Andrew at times, is a comic subplot in a larger drama. When I met him, my life was on course. I was happily married, my career was supporting my more successful external efforts developing a portfolio of rental properties and home rehabilitations. He was still learning his craft and wondering if he could survive in the dual role he played with his father. I watched a parade of beautiful women enter and leave his immediate circle.

I was there as he moved from a small Parsippany, NJ bungalow to a lake property in Morristown to a carriage house in West Orange. With each move, his energy and focus sharpened. Andrew is one of the few individuals who, as they aged, got physically stronger and more disciplined. As most of the rest of us were turning into sportsmen, Andy was becoming an athlete. I survived his forays into kickboxing, fencing, martial arts, and other physical challenges. I was there as one day he told me he had met HER. I had no doubt.

Andrew was one of the first people there as my wife, Susan, was diagnosed with cancer. As other people shied away, he showed at the front door with a gift. As the two of us bid goodbye to Susan, we retreated to the Delaware Water Gap for a fishing trip with my new fishing lures.

He was also one of the first to be there when Susan died.

I have had the wonderful fortune to have watched Andrew and Wendy grow together over the years feeding each other the nourishment of faith, commitment, and a true passion for life. Over twenty years, through all fortunes that life may pitch, I can't remember a time where the Jacobs household was not a positive force for each and everyone who may enter. This is the gift they have given their three children, Ben, Alex, and Kayla.

A couple of years ago, as my life was meeting another crossroads, I had been invited back to New Jersey as Andrew was contemplating a business expansion. With no other thought, I accepted and was soon on a plane ride east. I spent a week working in his office, meeting the talented team he had assembled and having them meet me. In the end, I looked into his eyes before returning to my new home in Utah. No other words were needed as I regretfully turned down his offer. I have never explained my decision to Andrew. In my career, I have made it an absolute, not to hire anyone that I could not let go if the need arose. I would never place the stress of making that decision on him. As it happens, as a friend, I came out well ahead in the long run… Andy, Thank you.

Since leaving New Jersey after Susan died, I have proven again to be the luckiest man on Earth… marrying Janet in the summer of 2000.

I first introduced Janet to the Jacobs in 1998 when Andy and his eldest son, Ben arrived in Utah for a camping trip with my brother Chuck and myself over the long Memorial Day weekend. I don't recall exactly what I had related to Andy regarding facilities and bugs. I am sure that I spoke of a plethora of one and a dearth of the other. Must have been a translation error. By this time, Andy knows me well enough that as soon as he says he is the best, I take it as a personal challenge. Hence, the Hearts marathon. Even as I beat him (and the others) with absolute aggressiveness, I doubt he learned a lesson. He will only make it more difficult for me the next time. (I hope it is soon)

The weather was cold for late spring in the mountains and the black bears were just coming out of hibernation as the ranger came into camp to warn us of a wounded bear in the immediate area. The actual counts of the facilities and bugs were quickly relegated to a lower priority. I very rarely trust others, Andrew being the exception, in my camp with a loaded 357, but as I laid down to sleep, I was confident all members of our party would awaken with the dawn.

In 1999, Janet and I went east for Ben's Bar Mitzvah. An amazing trip for us as a couple and for me, personally. Reacquainting myself with both sets of Andy's parents, friends, and his friend Dan the Rabbi; Janet and I sat with the family. I am sure it is a day that we will not forget. Janet was so impressed with the humanity and love she experienced at the Bar Mitzvah, she had asked if we could have Dan perform our wedding. So it is with all of the people that Andy and Wendy have introduced me.

With the greatest regret, Janet and I elected not to attend Alex's Mitzvah, celebrated shortly after the attack on New York. It is one of the few regrets in my life for decisions that I have made.

This missive could go on for many pages, but best I get to the point now... As previously noted, I have just completed Andrew's latest book. It arrived unsolicited late yesterday afternoon. Andy, everything you have said has been proven true. I sincerely love you, Wendy and the kids and look forward to celebrate Kayla's Bat Mitzvah with the families and friends. But, as you know, I never willingly cede the last word ...and never give up... and never be beaten...

Memoirs of a Sales Warrior:

PART I

"My Life"

Chapter 1

How I Got Started

6/3/2002

I was riding down the New Jersey Garden State Parkway in a combination of euphoria and disbelief. Our family owned company had just landed the biggest single piece of business in our company's history. My thoughts moved backward in time to when I first started in the business. I had gone to school to learn to be a broadcast journalist, when I did not get a job in my chosen field, in retrospect; I was not good enough. I was then left with a decision about what to do with my life.

People always said that I could sell so as I stood pondering in the kitchen of my parent's house, I decided to go into sales, walked into the next room and announced that fact to my Dad. He said if I gave up the idea of being a journalist then I could come work for him in the family printing business. Having few options I quickly agreed. It was June of 1977.

I did however, have some trepidations about joining him. Working for your father is giving him double power, both as boss and Dad. I was somewhat concerned, but as I said I had few options, at least that is what I thought, and he was willing to take a chance on me, so we both went for it.

After about 6 weeks in the business trying to learn everything as quickly as possible my Dad pointed to the door and said go sell. I said "Sell what?" He said, "Sell printing." I said "I did not know anything," I was twenty-one years old, had taken no printing courses in college and did not know an invoice from a shipping memo. He said "it doesn't matter," he gave me some samples, said to go knock on doors, ask for whomever bought the printing and bring back anything they gave me for a quote.

Not willing to admit fear and not ever wanting to fail at anything again, like not getting an anchor spot on the evening news, I took the samples and confidently went out of the office and out the front door. As I was walking through to the outside the thought suddenly occurred to me that I did not know what I was doing. I was going to knock on doors of people who did not want to see me, would probably be nasty and quite possibly have me thrown out. I was in for a gigantic amount of rejection and my world seemed to go gray. It was like I had walked through a portal and as I looked out in front of me, the wind started to blow, the skies got cloudy and I got very scared, how could I do this, how could I sell something I knew nothing about?

Panic was now setting in, I still hadn't moved from the front step of the building, and I mentally prepared myself to handle what was about to happen. "Use your experience" I told myself, "where else in your life have you been rejected a lot, with people who did not want to see you and in a hostile environment". And then it hit me, this situation was just like dating and as soon as I made the connection I had my answer.

Back when I was about fourteen years old and I wanted to start going out with girls, my dad took me aside and explained to me the one in three rule. For every three women he asked out, one would say yes. It did not necessarily happen with every third girl, sometimes he would ask out twenty with no luck and then streak with the next few, but over time, the rule proved out. He suggested that I keep it in mind when I started asking girls out, so that it would not crush me when I got turned down. The turn downs only meant that I was on my way to a success.

So I tested his rule and by the time I met my wonderful wife I had asked out over 600 women, 400 said no but about 200 said yes. It got to the point that I would ask out woman strictly to keep up my percentages. Knowing that the "1 out of 3" rule held I had asked out many types of woman and never ceased to have a lot of interesting experiences. I never got to like being turned down, but once you become "tournament tough," the negative responses begin to mean less and I could focus on the winners.

So there I had it, back at the front stoop, I did not know what the percentage in sales would be, maybe not 1 out of 3, but I was pretty sure the rule would hold. So now I could go out and knock on those doors, learn my craft and get a percentage of the winners, besides I could look for girls while doing it, which was an area I had already some success.

What I did not know was that my Dad was sending me out "cold calling" which meant knocking on doors with no appointments. It has the lowest percentage of success in terms of selling; normal rates are 1 or 2 out of 100 calls. My Dad did it to see if I had the guts and tenacity to continue so he could decide whether I was worth the effort to train. He was a tough boss, and it did not stop there either.

Luckily for me, I did not know the percentages of cold calling and I did not know how hard it was for most people because, as it turned out, I liked it. I enjoyed attacking companies with no appointments and I was good at it. I had my first order in about six weeks, I wasn't even doing it full time, and as the months passed I started to break the accounts my father and grandfather could not, which was a source of continuing joy. My Dad was convinced that I had the raw talent and brought me inside to learn my craft.

That was in 1977, I was twenty-one and am now forty-six years old, my Dad has fully retired. My sales helped to make his retirement a time of non-concern regarding money, and I now own our company. As time went on I grew to love sales and people in general. You cannot learn anything about selling from me if you do not have faith in what I have learned and what I did with the knowledge I attainted. Please read on, there are no hidden messages, so take these chapters for what they are, the result of a life of incredible experiences surrounded by my wonderful family in a work environment that is fun and stimulating, while also very tough and unforgiving.

Chapter 2

The Six Rules of Selling

12/19/2001

Selling cannot be learned in school or a laboratory, it is a skill that must be honed to a razor's edge if you are going to maximize your capabilities in the fields that you pursue. I can't be there to help you in person, but I can give you a structure that can get you started. This structure is based on my *Six Rules of Selling,* also known as my *Six Rules of Life* because they are so interwoven together that learning one means learning the other.

Rule #1

> *Selling is the exchange of goods and services between one person and another.*

In other words, whether it is going to the butcher, looking for a job, trying to sell your products or services, every time you contact another person, you are in a selling situation. Within that contact there is an exchange of energy, goods and or services and one of the two people will come out the better in the exchange. If one of them is smart enough, then they will both achieve what they want and be ready to enter into another contact to do more business.

Were you a high-school sports star? Most of us weren't and it is a good thing because we were not brought up with the "you owe me a great life" attitude. If you were not a star then, you could be one now. Selling doesn't just occur in business. Entering into relationships on various levels with people who have something that you want, and who you can supply something for them in return, is the essence of having fun and being successful. You don't have to be great looking; a star athlete or anything that is not already inside you, your basic human needs and desires will drive you where you need to be. It could be as simple as buying a pair of shoes, or closing a multi-million dollar deal. The concepts are the same.

Rule #2

> *You can never get what you want from someone else until you define first what they want and then satisfy their need. Only then will you have a chance of getting what you want in return.*

It is a simple concept but difficult to perform, in order to get what you want, you have to be willing to give first, otherwise nothing can get started.

I had a potential customer who I had been after for years. One Friday I got a purchase order in the mail with the due date for that Monday. I tried to call the customer to let him know we would have to work the weekend and overtime would be involved but he wasn't available. Fearing a late delivery more than having a problem with the money, we did the job and delivered it on time. As it turned out, the purchase order had been a test. The buyer had wanted to see how we would act under pressure and if we would come through for him especially if we had to make the decision about whether to go ahead or not. He became a good account and taught me a great lesson, when in doubt always act in what you think is in the best interest of the customer.

Rule #3

The most important thing to anybody, apart from their family, is their job. The 2nd most important thing is a better job.

When I first got out of college, I went to New York City to look for a job in broadcasting. I remember looking up at the gigantic buildings and realizing that no one in any of them cared if I lived or died. It was a turning point in my life because I did not want to be in any situation where I did not matter. Within a few hours, after I had returned to my parents' house in New Jersey, I decided to go into sales where everyone said I had the best chance of success.

Americans are defined by their work. If you are able to help someone to keep their job, through the good use of your products or services, or even get them a better one, then you are the person they want. Do not be naïve to think that their company's welfare comes before their own; people look out for themselves because no one else will.

Rule # 4

You are there to do business, never let your emotions get in the way of closing a deal.

Your wife is angry at you, your boss is making you work the weekend, layoffs are coming and you were the last one hired. Who cares about your problems? Certainly not your customer or anyone else you could be doing business with. If you have trouble in areas of your life like everyone else, your customer should be the last one to know about it. Your emotional baggage and problems are yours, do not share it with others, it is both unfair and irresponsible. Besides when given a choice no one, especially your customer, wants to hear about you unless it is good and affects them in a positive way.

Remember you are there to do business. Do not let your emotions get in the way of closing the deal and getting what you want. It is also irrelevant if you like the person you are dealing with or if you had a bad day. You have to stay focused on what you are doing and take care of your troubles on your own time.

Rule #5

If you are not prepared to put your life on the line then you will be beaten by someone who will.

I flew for the first time since 9/11 recently. I was apprehensive both about the heightened security at the airport and the overall danger of flying. When I got to the airport, not only was I asked for my proof of identification three times, but I was actually searched which included being "patted down" by a security guard. By the time I got on the plane I had already decided that this wasn't for me and I was planning to fly as little as possible from that time forward. But on the way back home, and going through security again, I realized that, first, it was necessary and second, it was now part of the game. The heightened security would not go away and unless I was willing to put my own fear behind me or I was going to be beaten by someone who would fly to see the customers I was afraid to visit.

What time do you get up in the morning? How much research do you do on your off hours? How well do you know your product lines? Commitment is everything. The customers are trying to keep their jobs and will place their confidence and business with those they feel are most capable and can be counted on, especially in times of trouble.

Rule #6

Failure is not weakness.

Listen UP! This is really important. No one expects anyone to bat 1.000% or win every game. You are working on percentages and if you can't take rejection, pressure and stress, then your level of success in every "selling" interaction will decrease proportionally. Ask any salesman about the percentages they get out of "cold calling" for leads either on the telephone or "door to door" and they will tell you they have about a two percent success rate. This means for every one hundred attempts, they will average two potential customers. There are other types of selling, like referral-based, that have a higher percentage, but even in the best cases, the odds are always against that you will make a sale.

The secret is in those odds; they will always work for or against you. If you make enough intelligent attempts then the percentages, which are dependent on your method and degree of ability, will always hold true. Being told no by a prospect simply means that you are moving further towards a yes. All it takes is time and determination, both of which you will only know after you test it out in real situations.

Failure is part of the game; it only becomes weakness when you give up. Selling is not a place for those who are not aggressive and who don't want to appear pushy. The reason there is so much money to be made in sales is because it is so difficult and takes a total life commitment.

Even if you don't "sell" for a living you are still "selling" all the time and since every interaction is a selling situation you might as well be as good at it as possible. Your goal should be to get the best out of every relationship for you and the other person so the relationship can continue.

Six Rules to change your life, they changed mine and are continuing to do so. The better you are at any of them, the more money you will make, the more successful you will become and the happier you will be in your relationships. They may seem simple, because they are, but they will lead you on a journey of self analysis and discovery that will allow you to attain all that you deserve as you are ready to handle it.

There you have it, my life in a nutshell.

How good are you at planning?

How much money do you want to be making by this time next year?

CHAPTER 3

The 2nd best way to learn how to do something, besides of course doing it yourself is to hear how someone else did it. That is why I am always suggesting that people read autobiographies, because you always want to read about someone who actually did something as opposed to someone else who gives you an untried theory.

Attack Now

10/3/2001

In real estate the three most important things are: 1) location, 2) location and 3) location. In selling the three most important things are: 1) attack, 2) attack and 3) attack.

Some people think that times right now are horrible. There is the tragedy of the World Trade Center and the Pentagon, the threats of more bombings and germ warfare. There is the frightening idea that our children may end up fighting in some foreign place that resembles more the face of the moon than the earth. The stock market is dropping, internet stocks have died, big business is laying off thousands of people, capital is drying up and people are feeling scared.

Have I depressed you yet? Don't be, because things are not nearly as bad as you may think. How do I know? The answer is history. My grandfather started our business in 1921, and when the Great Depression came times were very bad, but our family was fine. When World War II happened and shortages were rampant, we were fine. When Korea, Vietnam and a host of large and small recessions came and went, times were rough, but we were fine. Why, because we attacked!

When times are tough, customers are looking for better ways to do things to increase efficiency, save money and reduce manpower. When things are running well, the tendency for the customer is to have things stay as they are thereby keeping the door closed to the possibilities of you, a new vendor, getting more business.

Tough times are your invitation to increase your market share and elbow out your competition. It is your chance to show your creativity and how you can make your prospective customers look like stars in the eyes of their bosses and help them to hold their jobs.

Tough times are your windows of opportunity; like wartime in the military. It is your chance to rise through the ranks at unheard of speed because you have demonstrated that you have what it takes to get the job done, and do it better than your competition.

What do most people want when times are very bad? They want something or someone to believe in, they want to be associated with a winner. If your company is doing well in the face of incredibly bad business odds then you are the person they want to deal with.

How do you gain and hold this attitude?

It cannot be bravado; it has to be based on fact. Is your company financially solid? Can you hold out while other companies fold because of poor cash flow? Has your company ever been through hard times? Do you have a history of not only surviving but also thriving in difficult times? Do you know your product lines? Can you think quickly, and use your brain to come up with new ways to do things? Are you willing to put your heart, soul and mind on the line to help your customers fight through the problems at hand?

Make no mistake, we are all in battle, whether the military is used or not, the economy has put us into survival mode and if it comes down to who wins or loses I am willing to do anything necessary to survive and succeed, the question is, are you?

You are now fighting against the survivors; the marginal people are going out of business or being absorbed. If you are not ready for the fight then find someone who is and join them. Now is the time to soar like a comet through the night sky and accelerate your company ten times ahead of where it would be. This is the chance of a lifetime, rejoice, you have the ability to be a part of it! And remember to always attack.

How much money do you want to be making 5 years from now?

Chapter 4

We can learn from anyone-no matter what the age:

My Son's Friend Was Right

2/20/2002

My oldest son Ben, like every other young boy, did not want to listen to his father for advice about girls. I felt I had a vast pool of knowledge which reflected the experience of having suffered through many personal relationships, and I wanted to share them so he could avoid some of the pitfalls that I plunged into. But like all sons he did not want to listen, so I started to write down my thoughts just in case it might be easier for him to read it as opposed to listening to me.

Granted it sounds egotistical that I would consider myself an authority on dating, women and relationships, but my philosophy of using percentages to one's advantage, originally developed by my dad, worked incredibly well for me. That method ended with me meeting and marrying my wonderful wife so I felt I had something to contribute to the subject. As it turned out, after my son read my thoughts, he not only liked it, and thought I was a good writer, but began to distribute it to his friends. I became a sort of reference and sounding board when it came to going out and how "things" were progressing. My son and his friends are fifteen years old and while that might seem young to someone my age, for many of the kids today they are seasoned veterans in the game of dating.

I don't usually mind giving my kids rides for car pools, with the hectic life style we lead, it is often a good time for a little catching up and re-connecting. One night I was taking Ben and two of his friends to the next town where they were meeting my son's girlfriend, another girl (my son's ex girlfriend) and another friend of my son's girlfriend who was just a friend of the third boy. I hope this was clear because it is important to the rest of the story. The car conversation turned to my son's friend who was about to start dating my son's ex-girlfriend. As we drove they talked about how it was going so far. He had held her hand that morning at school and was hopefully going for a little more that night. When I queried whether that meant a kiss, he replied he hoped for more than one and then asked my counsel. I suggested taking it slowly because public displays of affection (PDA's) by a guy must be carefully planned. If he overplays his hand and moves too fast, the girl can get scared and it will set them back, as a couple, for weeks and perhaps permanently harm the relationship. He agreed with my assessment but was later somewhat miffed at my son for having told me of the circumstances in the first place. The non-attached girl for the other boy with us was not really girlfriend material so our conversation about him switched to the past New Year's Eve.

Apparently, late that night, he had ended up with the unusual chance of kissing three girls in rapid succession. Where the parents of the girl hosting the party were I do not know but apparently things were unsupervised at that point. My wife and I are perhaps a little overprotective on this point. The only time a girl

Ben's age slept over our house, we had Ben sleep in the basement and the girl slept upstairs chaperoned by us. Of course, that didn't matter as the lights were about to go out my younger son came walking out of her room after being there a ½ hour talking, without my wife and I knowing he was even there; so much for parental security.

Returning to the boy and New Years Eve, apparently he had to the chance to kiss at least one or more of the girls and decided to do nothing. He got razzed by the two boys as well as me saying he missed a golden opportunity, and that it was every male's dream to try and "make out" with more than one woman at the same time. But, in retrospect I was wrong, not just because of what could have happened if they said "yes" but even worse if they said "no", because the odds were not in his favor. It is hard enough being a teenage boy and being rejected by one girl in a romantic situation, how devastating it would be to be rejected by multiple woman at the same time? What do you say or do if they all say no? It could be a life changing experience, in a bad way. He had been right to pass, he was in an impossible situation and he took the only sensible, intelligent solution, and the next time I see him that is exactly what I will say to him. He was not ready to handle the worst case scenario-rejection. He knew there would be consequences. My sons' friend thought it out more than the three of us in the car and even though I am "the reference", in this case I still have a lot to learn.

How much money do you want to be making 10 years from now?

Chapter 5

Some dreams never die.

Today I Became a Roadie

2/25/2002

The fastest way to be cool while growing up in the 60's and 70's was to either be a sports star or in a rock band. Since I was neither good enough to be a great athlete and the clarinet has never and will never be considered a passkey into rock and roll respectability, I was determined to work my way up the ladder of life the old fashioned way, by hard work and my good looks. Okay, confidence was never a problem for me.

Nevertheless I was always a little bit jealous of rock stars and how they seemed to be a magnet to every good looking woman within 100 miles of wherever they were playing. This did not become relevant until my eldest son Ben decided he was going to learn guitar. I did not think much of it, especially since my good friend the Rabbi gave him his first instrument so he could learn enough to teach songs at our Temple. Little did any of us know that would it create a great passion that not only knocked out his previous idea of becoming a doctor, but now was replaced with being a full time musician.

As a parent I am not big on the idea as music as a career. Obviously the chance of making a decent living as a musician is not great. Being around large amounts of cigarettes, alcohol, drugs, and people with loose morals, plus bad hours, crummy living conditions and extremely loud music is not conducive to what I would call a happy life style. But a passion is a passion and part of my job as a Dad is to support my kids in whatever areas they love as long as they do their best to live up to their potential and not kill themselves while doing it. And Ben really loves his guitars. He plays them constantly, saves up his money to buy more and his band, whose name keeps changing too frequently to keep tabs on, is his social life, brotherhood and base of emotional operations.

I would normally be more concerned about his future career except that his grades are very good, he is incredibly responsible and one of the best people I know so I can live with a little music. He and his band had a "gig" in Boundbrook, New Jersey today and since it was not at night (I don't go out after 8:00PM) it was my turn to be the "roadie."

For those of you who are not related to rock band personnel, and who live a quieter existence than I, a roadie is a person who helps moves equipment, gives rides, money for food and in general watches out for the welfare of the musician, at least that is the job when you are "parental roadies" like my wife and I. Today's show was almost changed to 5:00PM on Sunday instead of 2:30PM but my wife and I put our foot down and told the kids they had to tell the music director of the café they were playing that 5:00PM was too late. I can just imagine the parents of the Beatles calling the Coliseum and telling them the concert is starting too late because Paul and Ringo have school tomorrow. But our son is not at that level, and too young to drive, so it was either 2:30 or no gig.

Actually this was the first time I watched my son and his two friends play together and they were good. I do not understand why they have to be so loud, but then I am not fifteen years old. The three girlfriends of the three band members were standing in the middle of the dance floor, hand in hand and watching their guys play their hearts out and it was a very cool scene.

As I write this I am waiting in the car for all of them to come out. I am taking all of the kids home since it is early. It is the least I can do since the other band parents often take the late shift. I am very fortunate to have a great son with really good friends who have fantastic parents. There could be a lot worse things in the world that they could be doing with their time and if they want to pursue their dreams, why not? It is nice to know that they are not ashamed of their parents and like having us around. It also gives me a chance to be a small part of a rock and roll band and see what it is really like.

Although the band does not make me cool or get me lots of girls, it does something much better which is a chance to support my son and be around him a little more before time passes and he leaves home for good.

How much money do you want to be making 25 years from now?

CHAPTER 6

There is an old saying that if someone isn't worrying then the company can't succeed. Dedication does not start at 9:00AM and stop at 5:00PM five days a week.

Sunday Night Again

3/11/2002

It is Sunday night again and I am due to get up at 4:00AM. The monsters are about to come out and force me into a night of worrying about not getting enough sleep and the panic that accompanies it. Ever since I was a child afraid of going to school the next day for not doing my homework, I would lie awake on Sunday nights and worry about what would happen if.... I used to worry about not doing well on tests, dealing with bullies, being drafted during the Vietnam war, I was ten years old, in short, everything. My incredible amount of energy, so useful to me in other areas of my life, was creating havoc at night when I was supposed to be sleeping. Of course watching horror movies on Sunday afternoons also did not help.

My older sister would go to bed, next my brother and then it would be just the sound of my parents' television and my wind-up alarm clock. 9 o'clock, 10 o'clock and finally 11 o'clock when their TV went silent and I would be left by myself. I would walk the hallways of our house and wander through the night. My parents referred to it as "night riding", the anxiety level so high I could not sleep and I roamed through the house like Paul Revere on his Midnight Ride. I would be so wired that nothing would allow me to pass out. The warnings by my mom that the longer I was up the worse I would function the next day only made things worse.

Therefore, for survival I learned a few things. First, I realized I needed less sleep then most people, and not getting a full eight hours on Sunday nights did not mean I would be a basket case on Monday. I also learned that watching horror movies was not in my best interest and stopped that practice permanently. One positive thing was discovering the benefits of exercise and that the more I got the better chance I had of falling asleep. If I was too tired to think then I was too tired to worry. This system helped reduce my stress in general and allowed me to fall asleep easier and be happier.

As the years went by I became a good student and then successful in business and kept increasing the amount of exercise always looking for the athletic "high" of being too tired to think, too sore to move, able to eat anything because the calories didn't matter and fall asleep anywhere. Luckily, my wonderful wife, seeing what I was doing to myself, tried to rid me of my anxiety ridden obsession and introduced me to yoga.

Unfortunately, meditation does not seem to help on Sunday nights, and here I am again. It is 9:58 and I have already told some of my kids to be quiet. I will have one small window of time within the next hour to get to sleep. If I miss it I will be up for hours and the mere thought of that causes anxiety and decreases my chances for sleep. I can hear the rest of the house shutting down around me like it did when I when I was a child.

I have a big week coming up with lots of great potential things happening and I am both apprehensive and excited, two emotions, again not conducive to being calm enough to sleep. But I would not change my life for anything and if going through the purgatory of Sunday nights is the only way I can earn the right to go back to work where I can influence my destiny and have a chance at my dreams then so be it.

I do not believe that you can put in 8 hours 5 days a week and run a business or be able to sell successfully. The commitment necessary to be able to succeed and meet your dreams and expectations far outweighs the societal norm of working a forty hour week. There are many people out there who are smarter and tougher than I am. The difference between us is my willingness and ability to accept stress and the commitment of time and energy to achieve goals over the long term.

Part of that sacrifice is the need to think about work, your position, and tactics for dealing with life in general and business, in particular, for many hours of the day often most days of the week. If you are not willing to commit the time and energy then you will be beaten by someone who is. It often means that it interrupts your sleep, vacations and chance to relax. If you decline the challenge then, on a percentage basis you will be beaten by someone more willing to do it like me.

But that also means that it is hard to shut off your mind which brings me back to Sunday nights. I love my life and am incredibly thankful for what I have. Perhaps if I ever retire, then this Sunday night ritual will fade into an amusing memory. But when my career ends and every day becomes indiscernible from the next, I will have lost something. They say the problem with retirement is you never get a day off. The thrill, foreboding, anxiety, anticipation and potential for all types of things will be missing. Every Sunday night is a battle. Occasionally I triumph but it is an ongoing struggle and one which I will engage in indefinitely because it is part of the price for the life that I cherish. It is now 10:39. Wish me luck I'm going to bed.

Chapter 7

There is no such thing as a dead end job. Whether it be waiter, garbage man or snow-shoveler. All tasks are worth doing well and a lot can be gained if you are open to the knowledge.

The Best

3/22/2001

Mr. Rich died last week, he was in his nineties.

We lived next door to him when I was growing up. From the time I was a little kid he always seemed old to me. He had a small, meticulously groomed mustache and carried himself with great authority and class. His house was filled with antiques and I especially admired his pocket-watch collection, which he displayed in glass cases in his living room. He seemed to live a life of dignity.

One day when I was young, probably about ten years old, I was suddenly declared the new snow shoveler for his driveway. I don't remember asking for the job; in fact I thought that my brother had the "contract." But nevertheless I became the heir apparent and my job was to make sure that if it snowed I was to be up early enough to do his driveway before I had to go to school.

You will notice that I left out doing our driveway before school. I was a capitalist from the moment I was born and it occurred to me that I should go where the money is so I naturally took care of my paying customers before my own. In those days, before political correctness and lawsuits many of us kids made money going door to door shoveling snow. Some of us were able to secure contracts and those snow days helped to extend my money supply way past my allowance. As time went on I took on a second contract, but that meant I had to get up really early and one time I got yelled at by the 2nd contract's husband because I was making too much noise too early in the morning. It was a big mistake for the husband because I threatened to leave the shoveling for him and things quickly returned to their profitable norm.

I learned many things from Mr. Rich like the benefits of getting up early which meant I had the best snow contracts which also meant I had my own money to spend. I found that I could do what others would not which meant that for a little less sleep I could get what I wanted, which was financial independence from my father. Being willing to get up early has meant a windfall for me because I was able to do what others could not. It was a symbol of my commitment to whatever I was doing and it always worked in my favor.

Mr. Rich also taught me how to shovel a driveway; it is not as simple as it sounds. Shoveling snow is like playing chess. You need to survey the situation, conditions and set-up your shoveling like a battle plan to insure that the snow is removed in the cleanest, most efficient fashion. You had to consider from which side of the street the plow would be pushing snow onto your newly cleaned area and which direction the wind drifts would be pushing those flakes you had toiled so hard to move.

Certain snow could be broomed, some had to be cut into pieces like for an igloo and still others could be pushed. These variant conditions sometimes called for different types of equipment, again taught to me by Mr. Rich. While he was showing me how to shovel he was also helping me to learn to think, plan and improvise when conditions changed, as happened often in winter and life.

He also taught me that there was no job that was not worth doing well; even shoveling snow could be done in a better way, almost to an art form. A beautifully shoveled driveway after a snowstorm was a picture of elegance and gave one a definite sense of accomplishment and purpose.

Later on when I was about to get married, I contacted Mr. Rich; he owned a very successful pawn shop and merchandise store. I asked him to show us some diamonds for my wife's engagement ring. She was expecting to see a wide array of diamonds so she could choose, Mr. Rich however came over and pulled out one diamond and said "This is it."

My wife looked at me helplessly, and after he turned away I said to accept his decision and I would get her another one later if she did not love it. He was an old family friend and I did not want to make a scene. But after a few weeks my future wife turned to me and said she loved the ring just as it was, he had been right again.

Mr. Rich taught me again, that by being definite and confident you could do things that others would never dream of. He thought he knew what was right for people and acted on his own, it did not matter what other people thought. In that vein I do not think I go as far as he did but I have also seen that well placed confidence, and being definite, can get you a long way towards being successful in selling and life.

I had not seen Mr. Rich for a few years but the memories of him had been burned in my mind. It is not often you meet someone who is unforgettable, he helped me in so many ways and I will always be grateful for the lessons he taught me, and that goes for whether I am conducting business or shoveling a driveway.

Now everyone thinks I am crazy for cleaning my own driveway, especially when I can pay someone else to do it. What possible motivation could there be? I race the plowing service to get out there so I can do it myself, because something inside me wants to prove I can still do it, being outside, taking on the elements and doing a better job than anyone else because I was taught by the best and I knew it.

Chapter 8

Did you ever have the feeling that you were be moved by forces beyond your control?

A Tribute to Ian Schneider

2/20/2002

My daughter called me yesterday and asked me to be an assistant coach for her town softball team this spring. My first answer was "no". I did not want to do it, commit to the time and I was never any good at softball anyway. My second reaction was that I was a jerk, my daughter was asking me to share some time and an activity that she liked and I had declined. I should have remembered that she was only going to be ten once in her life and how many opportunities like this would I get? I then said "I would love to do it, but to keep in mind I was lousy at the sport". She said "thanks dad," and hung up. It was only later that I realized how I had almost made a huge mistake by originally saying no.

Ian Schneider was one of the truly great soccer, baseball, every sport Dad coaches. If his kids played in a sport, and they played in a lot, then he or his wife were not only at every game, he usually coached it. His enthusiasm was contagious, his commitment total and his love for his kids, the game and life were eternal. To watch Ian coach was to view a master at work. He would have those nine year old girls, including my daughter, running, hitting, giggling and cheering no matter how cold, hot, dry or wet it was. He loved to win but with the kids it was all geared to having fun. His smile would light up the field and I would watch him in awe as the general who led a happy army.

Ian was killed when the World Trade Centers collapsed, the effects on his family were obviously devastating, but because of the man he was, those shock waves spread everywhere. I had been wondering how my daughter was going to handle playing softball again with Ian not being around. Even if she was not on his team his mere presence permeated all parts of the game and I worried how she and the rest of the kids, not to mention his own daughter, would handle it all.

I believe in fate and I believe that when a vacuum is created someone is destined to fill it. The only problem with me being the fill is that I have very little experience with the game of bats and balls. Growing up I played little league and my main memory is having a sadistic coach who seemed to hate the world. I learned to have disdain for many of the parents in the stands who took the sport way too seriously. As an assistant coach I am determined to make sure the kids have a great time, water to drink, hats on their head, sun block on their faces and no parents giving them a hard time.

I could never fill Ian's shoes regarding coaching; I don't even like the game, but I can match his devotion to the kids and try to make sure that, even though he isn't there, they still have a great time. Besides I know when the chips are down and I am in a tense situation and my head coach has gone to the bathroom, Ian will be there to help me. His commitment and passion had no boundaries through space or time and I will be listening. But just in case he is at his son's game that day, or his daughter is not on my team I am going to get a copy of the rule book, fast.

What day do you plan to retire?

What is your dream job?

Chapter 9

Being successful and being compulsive are not necessarily tied together-but in my case they are.

I Am Not Perfect

6/6/2002

Okay I screwed up, I admit it. I spent the last week setting up a deal with a customer, covering every possible variation and trying to make sure everything was perfect. I was supposed to call him to set-up the final meeting and I forgot to make the call. Yes, I forgot, nothing more dramatic than that and two hours later when I was going over my notes I realized my omission and went nuts. I tried to call the customer and e-mail him. I tried everything and finally I got word through his receptionist that I had missed "the deadline" and to call him tomorrow. I now had to endure the night beating myself over the head for not remembering to make the call.

My mistake caused a breach in the customer's trust and his faith in my abilities to do as I promised. It does not matter that the customer was being harsh. First, as the customer, he has the right to act anyway he wants, and second, it was my mistake. I envy the people who seem to breeze through life with an absence of guilt and responsibility. They forget to call people back, don't keep appointments, never do as they say and it doesn't seem to bother them. I, on the other hand try to be perfect and when I miss, and in this case, miss big, it is a giant deal that throws me into turmoil and I feel awful. All that preparatory work possibly thrown out the window because of one missed phone call.

It was like the time I was supposed to pick up my eldest son Ben at school, I am sure he doesn't even remember this, I was ten minutes late and he looked worried that something had happened to me. I felt awful that I made him worry. My misses are so infrequent I not only remember the circumstances, but also dwell on them way past their worth.

The more that people know you care, the more trust and responsibility they place on you and the more pressure I put on myself not to disappoint them. I can't change the way I am and I know that anyone can make a mistake but it causes me great distress before I can let it go. The only good that comes from my turmoil is I can relate to someone else's anguish when they mess up and try to help them feel better. I am the first one to forgive and tell people to forget about the mistake and I am the last to do it myself.

I cannot stop being hard on myself but at least I can enjoy the benefits which are mostly being in control of what happens around me and accept the fact that mistakes will happen, try to fix them immediately and probably be destined for another bad night.

NOTES

Chapter 10

Real men do cry. Real men do mourn. Real men are human, a concept most of us have trouble accepting.

Like Beings Travel Together

3/17/2001

I got a notice the other day from our town. It was for a renewal for a rabies tag for my dog. I naturally thought it was for our new dog, a very feisty male Bichon named Bailey, but it wasn't. It was for my old dog Hershey who we had to put down last spring-she was fourteen and a half years old.

Seeing the form that I had filled out fourteen times before, the memories suddenly rushed back to me and a lump formed in my throat. I really miss her, she was my dog. I trained her for hunting birds, even though after the first few years most of our outdoor activities were kept to running in fields and woods near our home. She was incredibly well disciplined, if I do say so myself, and I would revel in the praise from people of not only how beautiful she was but how well behaved.

Of course she was also no wimp and there were times when she would want her way and I mine, but as the years passed and we both grew older the bond strengthened even more. We knew what each other wanted and the telepathic link between us grew stronger.

Over the last few years as she slowed down and began to get sick, I eased up on the discipline, especially as she stopped trying to go through holes in the fence to visit the other neighbors dogs. She was a very sociable animal.

The last year was the toughest, and she grew more feeble and I knew the time was coming, the dread became worse. Sometimes I wondered if I had done the right thing to have her at all; becoming so close to an animal I knew at best would only be with me for fifteen years. But I shrugged off the feeling because the answer always came back a resounding "yes". She was my dog, my ultimate responsibility and it was a role I have always cherished.

After she was gone we had her cremated so we could spread the ashes in our backyard. It was my one last attempt to stay close. We had a service and my eldest son played his guitar and we were all very sad.

A few months ago my wife got another dog and since I had picked out Hershey it was her choice to get Bailey. We got him from another family who could not take care of him well and he loves our house, the kids and especially my wife — he has a home. Me, he could take or leave. I get the feeling the dog has decided that my Wife is his and I am an intruder on his turf. The jury is out but I have the feeling Bailey will eventually learn his place.

But every once in a while when I look out in the back yard I still think I glimpse Hershey, as she was when she was young, full of energy and beautiful and I invite her in for then and all time.

NOTES

CHAPTER 11

You have to Keep Going

Enough for Two

3/21/2002

I have never really mourned for anything in my life. What a happy thought, that no person or thing that close to me had ever passed on. Most of my relatives that had died were either old or lived far away and the others, while meaning a lot to me, seemed to have faded into memory somewhat easily, until Hershey.

She was a German Short Haired Pointer and lived until she was almost fifteen, pretty old for a dog her size and yes I did what most everyone else considered wrong when feeding her. She never liked dog food so I used to give her what I ate. I always figured if it was good enough for me then it was okay for her, she usually agreed. She never acted like a dog, loved to sleep on our bed, usually when we weren't there, and occasionally demanded space even when we were. You could tell by her facial expressions and actions that she felt she ruled the house, next to me, of course, and she did. She was mine, would do anything for me and even now that she is gone she is still with me.

Sometimes I cry when I think about her and when I look in our back yard, where her ashes are spread, I swear I can still see glimpses of her chasing squirrels and rabbits and looking like a racehorse shimmering in the sunlight, but through it all I always smile.

Then about a year later came Bailey the Bichon. I never liked small dogs; I never liked small dogs that yapped, especially those that did not take command well. I really don't like little dogs with a cocky attitude that think they own my wife and I am an intruder. He was supposed to be my wife's dog and he did have spunk. I also never particularly cared for spunk either, I also did not like that he could seemingly climb cabinets and leap onto counters and eat everything in sight. What was it with that dog and my cereal? More than once we have found him with his head stuck inside the box furiously trying to get loose before we caught him.

I was never close to him for the first year, I somehow felt it was a betrayal to Hershey, to like and get close to another dog. But then a few weeks ago I got sick. It was nothing major, just a twenty-four hour bug that not only kept me out of work for a day (highly unusual) but actually forced me to stay in bed. I was so weak it became a major decision about whether to make the effort to put on the radio. A trip to the bathroom was a formal expedition but through it all Bailey never left my side.

Did I mention he was a great sleeper? He stayed there with me all day, and it was during that time that I grew to love him. Like Hershey, he never left my side and like Hershey he is now mine, at least I will now share him with the rest of the family. I look at him differently now, he looks forward to me getting home and

I am happy to see him. He steals food but I generally don't get mad, even if it is my cereal. It is nice to know that there is enough love in my heart for two, now if I can only get him to stop climbing up those cabinets.

How much money would you make at your dream job?

Where would your dream job be?

Chapter 12

My wife never really thought much about my writing until I wrote this. To love, honor and cherish someone is an indescribable blessing. If you are truly lucky you realize what you have while you still have it.

The Wonders of Spandex

12/13/2001

This past summer my wife asked me if I wanted to go to a James Taylor Concert during the 4th of July weekend. I normally do not like concerts, the noise levels are always too high (I once used ear protection at a Yanni concert) and I do not like the smell of cigarettes, marijuana or stale beer. But the thought of being with my wonderful wife and hearing the fantastic voice of James Taylor was too much to resist and I gave her a resounding affirmative.

When we got to the concert, it was a sell-out and although early we still ended up at the top of the "lawn seating" at the PNC Arts Center in Holmdel. It was a wondrous night with a perfectly blue sky that turned into an incredible array of stars as the music continued throughout the evening.

I began to watch the people, one of the great activities for me at any concert especially one outdoors. This concert was unusual because the age group varied from little kids to people in their seventies and I was having a field day watching and listening to them.

There was a group of college kids behind us. One of the boys spent the whole concert loudly trying to make conversation and impress his date. The only thing certain to me was that he was a pain in the neck and judging from his date's reaction there was no chance he was going to get sex that night.

Speaking of sex, I am in wonderment of spandex. There was another couple who also looked like they were in college. The guy spent at least half an hour standing up with his girlfriend in front of a crowd of thousands, with his hand on her backside on the inside of her "skin-tight" pants. The following thoughts came to me: First, his hand must have gotten rather warm from all that body contact; second, that they loved the attention; third, how did he get his hand down there in the first place, the pants were that tight; and fourth, what would happen when she sat down? Would his hand go with it? And then I thought, just like the first couple behind me, this guy probably isn't going to get sex either because in my experience, the more a couple shows passion in public the less that goes on in their bedroom.

My wife was having a great time, singing and swaying to the music, laughing and smiling. She was in heaven and it was great just being there with her. Our three kids had all gone away for the summer and we had gone back to "dating." It was like having a girlfriend again but without the pressure to talk all the time, think up witty things to say and be nervous.

The concert ended and on the way home, my wife told me about the wonders of spandex (it stretches), so at least one mystery was solved as to how that guy got his hand down there.

I will never ask my wife to wear tight fitting clothes in public nor will I ever stick my hand down her spandex pants in front of anyone else let alone strangers. Commitment means more than a ridiculous, public display of affection. It is about respect and devotion with knowledge and faith in the long haul that can lead you to the magic of a beautiful summer's night, the music of James Taylor and falling in love with your wife… again.

What skills would you need for your dream job?

____

____

____

____

____

____

____

____

____

____

____

What is your idea of the most suitable mate?

Age: ______________________________

Sex: ______________________________

Income: ______________________________

Location: ______________________________

Occupation: ______________________________

Best traits: ______________________________

Worst traits: ______________________________

Chapter 13

What makes someone "good" in sales? If everyone thinks you are doing the right thing is it right or should you go against the flow? I feel much more secure when people think I am wrong.

Good—They Say I Am Nuts

5/9/2001

My eldest son Ben and I were driving home, talking about the new manufacturing center we had just moved into and he said he was proud of me. Can you believe that? My son is a teenager, almost fifteen years old and he said he was proud of me. What a fantastic thing to say to anyone let alone a son to his father, I almost cried.

I had been working on finding a new place for our company for almost a year and it had finally happened the week before. I got my new set of keys, turned in my old ones and there we were, with three times the space, increased operational overhead and the potential to expand our business many times. I was feeling scared, proud, humbled, terrified. I was hiring more people, increasing the overhead and creating even more stress for myself and I was still incredibly happy because I was working on my dream.

Having a dream is what makes us all go to incredible lengths to see if we can make it come true - or at least some parts of it. In my case it took a great deal of looking for a suitable place, negotiations and finally lots of money and effort for all concerned.

I have been so stressed by the whole ordeal that, when given the chance, I decided to start training for a triathlon event to benefit cancer. I figured that with all of my nervous energy I should do something positive with it. Besides, it helped cut down on the intensity of panic attacks that came as the new space was being readied.

As our renovations of the new space progressed the stock market dropped and as our bills mounted many of the largest corporations in the country laid people off. I had figured that this would happen. All economies are cyclical and it was time for a downturn but how bad a drop, no one could know. I am not a genius, just a student of our company's history and I figured that in a downturn many of our competitors, who are working on slim cash resources, would have to go out of business and new opportunities would open up for us. Historically, during tougher times that has indeed happened. The manufacturing base in our country is getting older, consolidating and going out of business and the result is that overall production capacity is declining, offering us entry into new potential markets because "stuff still has to be made".

Throughout Ideal Jacob's eighty-year history this cycle has happened time and again so I was confident in making the move and expansion regardless of the current business climate. Whether or not I was right was the big question and might remain unanswered for quite some time. When I asked my Dad's opinion of our plans he said "It doesn't really matter what happens in the market place." If I wanted to expand and I was willing to work incredibly hard to make it successful, that alone was reason enough to do it.

Unfortunately, the right dreams are those that go against the flow of what everyone else thinks is a good idea so you find that you are constantly swimming alone and against the tide. It always feels more comfortable and safer to be going with the flow of the crowd and the general idea of what is thought to be the right path but it is seldom effective if you want to be successful and profitable.

After so much swimming I have gotten to the point where I feel much more comfortable with people telling me I am crazy than when they tell me I'm doing the right thing. I think it is a normal reaction to having been on the road for years building my sales from nothing.

Even after all that time and the success I have achieved the doubts always linger in the background, especially on Sunday nights when I think about the week ahead and begin to worry - what if something goes wrong or doesn't happen the way I think it will? Eventually I calm myself with the idea that on a percentage basis most of my plans will not work out the way *I thought* but that they have a way of moving me forward as long as I stick with my dream.

Since nobody knows what will happen in the future you have to go through the non-workable plans to get to the brass ring. It is a continuing ladder of growth that you can never stop climbing until you retire, decide you are okay where you are and stop, or die trying. Without climbing the next rung, you can never get to your next stage, whatever that is. It is a wonderful journey and the best and worst part is that you don't know what is around the next corner.

Having an incredibly supportive family makes it much easier, but in the end, on every Sunday night, I am left always alone with the occasional panic attacks and the recollection of the person who looked at our new location and said with a sneer " I thought they said this was a big place?" The world is full of people who will ground you whether your feet are in the clouds or planted deeply below surface, so be happy when they say you are nuts because it is your next step towards success.

Chapter 14

Did I mention I have a very patient wife?

I Am Driving My Wife Crazy

7/19/2001

Back in January I began training for "it"—a triathlon in Montauk, New York that was scheduled for a recently past Saturday in June. It is a charity event to benefit the Leukemia and Lymphoma Society and I got involved with it because a friend who has been doing bicycle marathons for years invited me to compete. In the past, my company has been a sponsor of his events and since I was experiencing a great deal of stress from the move and expansion of my business I thought it might be a good diversion for me.

Before I started training for the event I used to exercise once a day except for Sunday's when I worked out more. In order to get ready for this race, I decided to increase my workouts to an average of ten times per week which, in addition to making an incredible amount of laundry, meant that I was now exercising at least thirteen hours a week. The diversion had become an obsession and affected all those near me.

The triathlon consisted of a one-mile swim, a 6.2-mile run and a twenty-mile bike ride. When I first started out on this quest, I did not think it would be a giant deal. I figured that I would work out more than usual, the day would come, I would go and do it, not finish and that would be the end of it. Walking and mountain biking were often part of my weekly routine, but I have done virtually no swimming for the past thirty years. I can't run long distances because my knees don't like it and being on a bike for more than ten miles hurts my backside. The first time I got back into a pool, my son, a member of his high school swim team, had to re-teach me how to do it. This all added up to trouble when I thought about actually racing so I decided just finishing the entire circuit would be an accomplishment.

When I was asked what my best event was I had to truthfully answer that I was lousy at all of them. If I used my best projected times for everything then I would have finished in about four and one half-hours. The only problem was that the race officials pull everyone off the route after three hours and fifty minutes. It was clear that finishing the race was not an option and I decided it didn't matter. I had resolved that my participation was going to be my way of handling the pressure I felt from managing my business expansion and whatever happened that day was fine.

I set myself a goal to finish the one-mile swim. When I started training I could barely do 150 yards (3 laps in an Olympic pool) and the event requires swimming the equivalent of 72 laps. The event organizers provide kayaks on the lake that swimmers can legally hang onto in case of trouble. I felt that if I could finish the swim then everything else I accomplished would be gravy. I might be able to complete the 6.2 mile run (for me run/walk) but I wasn't looking past that to the 22 mile bike ride.

From early on I decided on some basic rules for myself. The first was that I was not going to permanently cripple myself just to try and finish it. When I got too tired to go on (when I could not walk anymore) I would stop. The second rule was that I was not going to hurt myself preparing for it. That meant I did very little running while training (none on asphalt) and I instead concentrated on increasing my overall endurance and energy by playing a lot of tennis, walking, exercising in the gym in my office, working on my swimming and taking yoga. I was confident that at the very least, I would not end up on race day being dead before I started.

I still had some major concerns about race day. The biggest was that I might sink during the swim, even though I knew I would be in a wetsuit in a salt lake and that the extra buoyancy would reduce (not eliminate) the chances of sinking to the bottom. I would like to publicly apologize to my son for any embarrassment I caused by wearing a full wet suit to the inside pool of our local Y. I know I looked out of place but I had to practice with it and besides, my wife likes "the look." I also want to thank my very good friend, Jerry, for the use of his outdoor pool and apologize to his dog Gus because he could not come out and play while I practiced. All the training went well and I even began to like swimming.

I wasn't sure how well I would hold up to the overall training regimen. I was sore most of the time and if I sat too long in one place I had trouble getting up but I am forty-five years old and those things might have happened anyway. At least now I could chalk it up to something positive. Whenever there was a block of time anywhere in my schedule I would exercise and keep contributing to a never disappearing mountain of laundry at home.

I was sure that I would never forget the weekend of the race and all of the actual events, but I also knew that the most important part was already done. The training, in addition to getting me to the best shape of my life and lessening my obsession with my weight, was a great release for much of the tension and stress that accompanied the half year process of preparing and actually moving our company.

For me, the by-product of the stress and strain was an incredible supply of continuous energy that had to be channeled somewhere, especially if I wanted to get to sleep at night. I chose to use the triathlon for that release and thankfully my wife chose to support that decision and for that I will be forever grateful. We also agreed we were ready for it to be over.

The week before the event, I came down with the flu and was unable to compete. Being a strong believer in fate, I have a feeling that I was being told not to go because something bad would have happened. But I accomplished a lot. I trained for five months, raised a lot of money and was able to see how far I could push myself physically. It pays to recognize your limitations and keep your goals within doable means so I know I will never do this again. I do not think I have limitations with my mind but I obviously have them with my body and pushing it past its limit, possibly contributing to my illness, was just plain stupid.

Knowing yourself, your strengths, weaknesses and limitations is a good thing, and pushing past them one level at a time is great but trying to totally redefine yourself all at once can be a disaster. I will never have a washboard stomach or abs of steel. But if you are lucky you get the flu before you kill yourself trying.

Notes

Chapter 15

Knowing yourself is one of the hardest parts of learning to sell. Why do you do what you do? Why do you seek the praise of certain people? Why do you feel you have to beat others? When do you know that you "did it?"

Who Counts?

8/8/2001

Part of accomplishing personal advancement is arriving at the understanding that you have chosen a standard by which you judge yourself. You set up a group of rules and guidelines by which you run your life and rate yourself as to how well you are doing and measure how far you have come.

Unfortunately, I have set impossible goals that can never be met, which means that I, like too many others, are destined to stay in a mindset of permanent non-fulfillment. I don't mean material goals like wanting to be a millionaire, or meeting the guy or girl of your dreams, getting married, having the home you want and kids who grow up to be whatever they choose. I am talking about those impossible goals, like getting the recognition we all crave from people who are unwilling or unable to give us what we want. In my case, it is a particular acknowledgement that I wanted from my father.

He grew up under his dad, my grandfather, an extremely capable businessman who started with virtually nothing and ended his life financially successful. My dad went into his father's business and I am the third generation to take over. I am sure from the way my dad speaks about my grandfather that he never said many positive things to him and without a doubt, never told him he was proud of his accomplishments.

So I was confronted with the legacy of my father, born in the Depression, who was always worried about growing a company too fast, getting too big, letting the overhead creep up and bite him from behind. The apprenticeship he served under his father ingrained an aversion to risking what he already had, a vehicle for insuring a comfortable living to care for his wife and family.

Neither my grandfather nor my dad had a passion for business - they did not love it. The triumphs and day-to-day disasters and the ability to maneuver through or around them was a never a battle either of them enjoyed. They worked because they had to and as soon as they could they moved onto something else.

I, on the other hand was incredibly fortunate to be born into a family business that I loved, was good at and still eagerly embrace everyday. I also have an amazing amount of positive energy that flows through me almost all of the time. That energy was a gift, something I did not earn and I believe it means that I also have an additional responsibility to utilize it in the best way possible.

I went into the family business because my father was the only one willing to give me a chance when I got out of college. I worked very hard and helped him to make a lot of money so he could retire and do the things he loved.

We have dinner once a week and he rarely wants to hear how the business is doing. The fact that I am expanding our operations, increasing the overhead and I am taking more risks only makes him more nervous instead of proud. In fact, the words that I want to hear most, "Son I am proud of what you have done and I am proud of you" can never pass his lips because my view of success and his are different.

I have put myself into a permanent state of frustration and anger because this is one of the few things I cannot achieve and there is nothing I can do about it. Prompting him to say something would negate its benefits. I am in a hole from which I can never emerge.

Or can I? The other day my eldest son, out of the blue, turned to me and said, "Dad I am proud of you and all that you are doing." I looked at him and almost started to cry because I realized that I had been looking to the wrong person for affirmation of what I had accomplished. My father will never say what I want to hear but my son did and in many ways it is more important to me and means a lot more.

We have the power to choose the opinions that "count" and what they mean to us. Much of our frustration in life comes from our inability to choose to listen to the right people. Just because someone is your parent, boss or has a special relationship does not give him the automatic right to judge you. You and I give them the power to hold judgment over us and it is up to us to choose wisely because that is the one area in our lives over which we have total control.

I love my dad, but I am not waiting for him anymore.

Chapter 16

I believe in reincarnation and that there are a lot of things we do not understand. I also believe that if you are open to new ideas then all kinds of things can happen.

It Pays To Be Nice To Everybody

4/2/2002

One of the most valuable pieces of advice I ever got from my dad/boss was to be nice to everybody. It seems too simple and so biblical to be practical and many people ignore it because it often takes a little effort. A "good morning" here, a smile there and a look of acknowledging that someone is human does take some energy but gives so much in return.

I play a lot of tennis and I belong to a local club. I often play very early in the morning which means I see the maintenance staff much more than most other members. They are a nice group of guys and since I am pleasant to them they are the same to me and it adds an extra dimension of "niceness" to my time there.

As it turned out it added a lot more.

A few months ago on my first flight after 9/11 I was in a security line at the airport. There were guards with guns and it was a pretty frightening experience. It was scary right up to the point when I was about to be searched by, you guessed it, a man who used to work at my tennis club. What could have been an intimidating experience turned into a neutral one because he smiled, I smiled, and the "pat down" of my body was at least being done by someone I knew.

In my family there is a great incidence of prostate cancer. Stay with me here - I know this is a weird segue, and it is going to get a lot stranger. Since there is a history I have myself checked regularly and during the previous year my PSA (potential cancer test indicator) was rising and I was getting scared. The doctor told me to come back in six months and as I left the office I knew I was going to have to do something other than just worry.

I resolved to try and modify my life, physically and mentally and bolster my body's immune defenses to fight whatever could potentially harm me. This included continuing with yoga, a slight change in diet, and a renewed effort to increase my positive mental attitude towards everything.

At this time I was reading a book by an intuitive healer who claimed that he could, by the energy transfer of his mind and touch, heal people with all types of ailments. In addition he said he could release souls of people who had died tragically and were trapped at the site of their death. Most people would not have given it much thought but I was ready to try anything to help myself. I remembered that at my tennis club a little boy had drowned the past summer in the swimming pool. It occurred to me that since he died tragically his soul may not be able to be released from the site and if he was stuck then maybe this man could help. I made a deal with myself. I would contact this man, ask him for help with my potential problem and in return if my PSA levels stayed the same or went down then I would try and find out about the little boy and help his soul get released.

When you have the potential of a life-threatening situation facing your seemingly way-out options begin to not look so strange. I called the healer on the phone (e-mail me if you want his name), and he spoke to me for a while and that was it. I would not know for six months whether it helped or not.

Six months was up two weeks ago and I went to the doctor for a blood test. My PSA level went down slightly!!!! Was it due to the healer? Maybe yes or maybe no but it was now up to me to complete the other part of the deal – providing the information about the little boy. At this point, as fate would have it, I got a mailing from the healer; he was coming to New York the next weekend and I would have my chance to see him in person and to help the little boy but I had to find out his name.

I went to the people I knew at the tennis club and no one wanted to talk about it. They did not want to think about the little boy's death, which I could easily understand, and they wanted it left alone. I was at a brick wall until I talked with one of the maintenance guys who called his boss. He was able to get me the first name, Ola.

I am scheduled to go into Manhattan this Saturday and I am armed with the little boy's name and the place it happened. I hope it is enough, but if not, I will check the local newspapers and find out whatever is necessary to try and help.

Most people want to do good things, and if you let them help they will think better of you. Selling is being able to communicate to people and fulfilling their needs so you can get what you want. The best salesmen are those who can give others what they want and get what they want in return and keep the relationship going. Selling is not relegated only to business, it happens everywhere with everyone you meet. I have no idea what will happen to me in Manhattan this Saturday but I am on a course that was pre-set by someone else and I can't wait to see what results. Hopefully it is for the betterment of us all.

Chapter 17

Here's more on that!

The Journey Continues

4/8/2002

I had to increase the odds of the healer or medical intuitive, as he is also known, of being able to help the little boy by getting more information then just a first name and the approximate date of the accident. I then remembered that I had a friend who volunteered at the local police department and I thought he might be able to access their records to find me more information.

When I called him, he thought I was nuts, surprisingly, he was the only person to react that way. He was not sure he could help me but said he had seen an article about the drowning in the local paper and I could call them for more information. I then called the paper who told me how to access their records and for about $7.00 I was able to get copy of the article! I had the boys full name, the date and all of the details necessary for the healer to zero in; at least I hoped I did.

I also called my Dad, and asked him if he wanted to go into New York with me. Although very set in his ways in certain areas he is also very progressive in others and did not hesitate to answer in the affirmative. So there we were on that Saturday morning on our way into Manhattan on the train, my Dad and I on a date with some type of destiny.

When we got to the hotel no one had any record of the man we were to see or the healing session he was to be running, but the head of security gave me a mysterious look and suggested we got to the Murray Hill room on the fourth floor. By this time nothing seemed strange so my Dad went up to the floor and sure enough there were signs for the healing session. When we signed in there was a release form, including affirming that we were not part of any government agency there to monitor his operation.

The group seated along a wall was a mixture of old and young, all types of nationalities and all of us including my Dad and I looked a little nervous. We were brought into a large room with about 25 beds and all of us were instructed to take off our shoes and sit on the beds with our eyes closed and facing the person across from us. Some of the people in the room were obviously in very poor health and others seemed fine. All of us were there were reaching out for something different than our current medical community had to offer which is why there may have been concern about government intervention.

New age music was playing softly and we were then told to lie down on the bed and put the blankets over ourselves and keep our eyes closed. A feeling of calm and tranquility enveloped throughout the room and as the music grew louder the healer went from bed to bed putting his hands on our foreheads, chests and necks. He did this several times through the next hour and half. Once I felt like I could see him through my eyelids as he came near me. I could hear the people around me going in and out of various levels of consciousness and I too felt myself in falling in and out of some type of sleepy state. For someone like me staying one place for more than twenty minutes is often torture but I did not get restless until more than an hour and half later.

Towards the end he came and spoke to everyone and when he got to me he asked me why I was there. I have rarely encountered such a calm, nice man, with a total outpouring of warmth. I told him I was there for general prevention and he mentioned that I was in good shape, although some of my "lines" were crooked but seemed okay. I assumed he was talking about the lines of energy going through my body and he then put his hand on my chest and asked if I felt anything. I said it seemed like there was power emitting throughout my body radiating from his touch and he said that it was good, wished me well, gave me a crystal to match the other one I had from him and went to the next person.

As I was leaving I left the envelope with the story I wrote about the little boy and the newspaper article with his assistant. I resolved to follow-up to see if he could do anything.

Afterwards my Dad and I both had the same reaction to what we had experienced, which was we did not know if it did any good, but since it was not invasive we did not see what harm it could have done. Some people would probably complain that any good was just a placebo affect. But in many studies the placebo affect can affect more than 5% of the participants. Think about it, more than one in twenty people can heal themselves just by thinking they are getting better. If this healer could help engage that productive energy without drugs or invasive surgery than he was my kind of guy.

I learned a lot about myself and my dad from this. When I first started I was prepared to be labeled a "kook" or "nut", but almost everyone was not only receptive but also supportive. Being sick and the thought of death is something that none of us ever really gets completely out of our minds. If there is a weird way to make our lives better, then ridiculing the unknown is a luxury that few of us have, when the chance for help may be out there.

My next PSA test is not for another 6 months but I am going for an ultrasound to create a baseline so we can see how well or not my body is doing from this point on. I am at the age, 46 years old, when the culmination of the various adventures of my years can start to have negative or positive effects. I am not one to sit by and wait for bad things to happen, especially when I feel I can influence almost anything. There is a lot we know nothing about, especially when it comes to energy transfers between people and things in particular and healing in general. I am not afraid to tell people where I am going, even if it is just to awaken the powers that reside inside myself which could not be released by me alone.

I woke up the next morning with a mark on my neck, one of the places where the healer had touched me. My wife swears it was not her so I am left with the feeling that the transfer of energy of the healer had actually happened. As for the little boy, I am now in possession of another crystal, the first of which I now wear around my neck. As soon as I can get back into the outdoor tennis area I will plant it in the garden next to the pool where the accident happened, maybe it will help somehow.

NOTES

Chapter 18

What are you afraid of? I know what scares me.

Belly to Belly

2/11/2002

My Dad always said you have to see the customers in person, nothing replaces personal contact. This was in my mind as I went to the airport for a business trip this morning for the first time since 9/11/01. I was a little scared at the idea of flying, after all, who knew what else could happen? I wanted to make sure that I would not be delayed by security and risk missing my plane so I put on a jacket and tie figuring that the security people would stop only people who fit a certain profile. For some reason I thought that a white, middle-aged (oh how I hate that term) good-looking (makes up for the middle aged) well-dressed man would be the last person they would stop and search. It was at the x-ray machine that I saw the first armed soldier. He looked very intimidating carrying an automatic weapon and no smile.

So much for my best laid plans, I got singled out for a random check but as luck would have it I knew the security guard. He was very pleasant while he put the metal wand around my body and actually let me know when he was going to "pat" down my shoulders and other areas of my body before he did it. He could not have been nicer but it was still unsettling. When I got to the terminal area I saw the second armed soldier and then a third and forth. By this time I was just hoping to get onto the plane, get to my destination so I could have the meeting, see my other appointments and come home.

But then I remembered what President Bush had said. He reminded people not to be intimidated by the terrorists, not let them change our way of doing things. The best way we could fight back was to keep going and do what we had to do. It was then that I realized the rules had been changed and that I had to continue making these kinds of trips. I just had to be more careful and realize that traveling, while never something I really looked forward to, had become a little more difficult and a little less pleasant.

If I expected to stay in the game I had to follow the rules. Otherwise I could stay home and never see the customers I could only see by taking airplanes. But that would mean the eventual loss of the business because eventually, it would be won over by a competitor that would accept the airport problems, was more dedicated to the customers, had a higher commitment level to his business and deserved it more than I.

So I was at a crossroads, accept what has happened, give up, cower and let someone else take my customers or fight back in my own small way. On the way back I started getting used to all of the soldiers, their guns and their presence and by the time I got back into New Jersey I was actually starting to feel better having them around. Better to be slowed up a little, get personally searched and maybe stop a terrorist then go back to being unaware and a sitting duck.

I never loved to travel before and I like it even less now but nobody, especially some insane madman half way across the world, is going to stop me from doing business and carrying on with my life. Who knows with more business traveling I might save up enough air miles to go on vacation somewhere exotic and I will go by plane.

If you could live anywhere, what would be your dream location?

What aspects of your dream location make it your dream?

Chapter 19

Energy is energy. Whether it is positive or negative you can train yourself to use it to your advantage.

Thanks, Dad

1/21/2002

You had to have seen my father in action to really understand him. Back in his glory days, those years when he was in his "selling prime" you could see the fire in his eyes when he spoke about business in general and sales in particular.

My Dad always had very definite ideas about what worked and what didn't in business and life. When I came to work in the family company he began to train me for business and sales and there were rules set-up that I was not only expected to follow but I had better adhere to or experience his wrath.

My Dad was a smart businessman and he loved not only molding me, but watching me grow to become the salesman he believed I could be. He knew that if I could become a successful salesman then not only would the family business survive to a third generation, but he could potentially make a lot of money. The only problem was that I did not agree with some (a lot) of his ideas on business and selling but I was told that nothing I said was of any worth until I proved myself by my sales. You were worth nothing until you could back up your opinion with cold hard money; it was the profit that mattered.

My Dad always taught me that you could not sell only the tougher, more unusual jobs to customers, you had to offer a whole line of products so you would be cemented into a continuing, long term relationship that would insure continual contact. That contact naturally put you into position for any new items that came up which gave him the chance to expand into new niche markets and profitable areas. It made sense and my Dad's method to accomplish this was to make weekly and monthly calls to customers on regular routes that he kept up for years. He would go out "selling" two or three days a week, see customers and take them to lunch. They always liked the fact they could count on seeing him regularly in person or any other time they desired. He loved his days out selling and was a permanent fixture in his clients business lives, a constant in a fast changing market place and it worked well for everyone.

Everyone, of course except me. The idea of weekly calls, stopping by to see people who often were not there, always seemed like an extremely inefficient use of time and I always felt I accomplished much more using the telephone. But, my Dad was the boss, besides being my father, a very powerful duo of positions, and I did what I was told. I made the regular calls and they worked and I began to build up my sales. But as I did that I started putting aside some time to try out my theories about business which was only going after the tougher, most unusual areas. As it turned out, for me, the regular calls were not the best use of my time and I was able to build a much bigger business by not being the "man for everything" but the supplier who is there when the going got tough and the pressure was at its hardest.

As my sales surpassed my Dad's and his numbers eventually wound down he never really thought much of the way I did things. I could tell he was always wondering when the work process I developed would peter out and I would have to go back to his way of doing things. In fact, he often thought little of my ideas and declared his pessimism that he did not think my plans had much of a chance to work. It got to the point that when I needed to be revved up about a new projects I would talk to him about it so I could be told it could not be done. Once I heard that, I became so determined to succeed that I am sure the odds of my success sky rocketed because I was out to prove him wrong.

Sure enough, last night at dinner, my Dad, who, had been totally out of the business for three years, listened as I told him about a new marketing plan, one which I was not sure I was going to use. He started telling me about all the reasons why it would not work and I got that "old" feeling again that it was time to prove him wrong.

I cannot tell you how many accounts and pieces of business I have gotten simply because my Dad expressed pessimism or certainty that it could not be done. Proving him wrong was almost as much fun as getting the actual business, almost.

So my Dad has done it for me again, he has motivated me far past what life, or probably even my guts could have, and I am off and running to prove him wrong. Thanks Dad, you are still helping me to win.

CHAPTER 20

If you are lucky enough to have a mentor, make sure to treasure them for as long as they last because, if they are good, they will not be around forever.

Mentors Are Not Perfect

1/10/2002

When I was growing up, I was not a good student. I used to watch incredible amounts of television and then would stay up on Sunday nights and worry because I was not prepared for what was coming the next Monday. I hated school, studying, and I especially hated Sunday nights. When I was in the 6th grade my Dad laid down the law and installed a set of guidelines regarding school that changed my life forever.

No longer was television going to be the center of my universe, knowing numerous tobacco commercials by heart was going to be replaced by grammar and math equations. My afternoons, instead of watching mindless junk, were now to be filled with my studies and nothing else would take priority.

It was a hard transition but I quickly realized what my Dad was trying to instill in me. It became crystal clear that it was much better to worry about whether you were going to get an "A" or a "B" then worry if you would pass at all. The structure he set down for me eventually became chiseled in stone and I incorporated it in other areas of my life.

I used to be a chubby kid when I was young, you know the type. I had to wear the "hefty" sizes in pants and I would always change the subject when weight was discussed among my friends because I was embarrassed. I realized that very few fat people in junior high school were cool and that the boys in shape were most likely to get the girls. It became painfully clear that if I was going to compete I needed to be fit in all areas, which included my mind, body and soul.

I learned what to do and the structure I created for my life served me well. I got into the college I wanted and graduated with the degree I longed for in broadcast journalism and then went out to find a job. Unfortunately, getting my degree was one thing, finding a place in the field was quite another. I never did get a job in television or radio and soon realized I needed a career path change.

When I decided to go into sales my dad suggested I work for him. Not knowing where else to go and grateful for not only the offer but the immediate raise in status of being employed, and the boss' son, I readily agreed. And with that, the second stage for my mentor, my dad, began. His tactics were draconian, his manner often brusque and his philosophy unbending. I did it his way, and in the end the final score card would tally how much I sold. He taught me his way in sales and business, no other way was tolerated. "Learn my way first", he said, then you can branch out on your own. As a true mentor he taught me and I absorbed it like a sponge. There was no way I was going to fail at this, no matter how he spoke to me or what he told me to do. I did what was expected and more and bided my time until I could go off and try things on my own.

In the best of all worlds you can give back to your mentor. In exchange for their experience and guidance you can give them something they, too, want and need like support, companionship or money. The best relationships are symbiotic, where both gain and grow together and for my first fifteen years in business my dad and I had just that. In exchange for teaching me all he knew about business and sales I gave my dad the chance to see his son develop and grow in the business he created. He got to see how far his philosophy and ideas could be taken and in the process I supported him in all areas and helped to make him a wealthy man.

As with all mentor relationships, when my dad was not able to give any more and my sales eclipsed his, what he got back began to wane and he came to see me more as a rival than his protégé until he eventually reached his end and retired. I often think back on how I would have handled it differently if I were my dad. How I might have gotten more joy out of the process and made it an easier time for both of us.

But mentors are not meant to be perfect, and the journey is not supposed to be without bumps in the road. The relationship by definition has to based on a time frame. The protégé eventually has to go off on his own or he will never optimize his capabilities. This doesn't mean that the mentor or protégé are bad people, it is simply time for them both to move on.

It is hard along the way not to think of your mentors as perfect. They seem to have all the answers for such a long time, that when you realize that they are human, have flaws, and are not the best at what they do, you feel resentment and can be disappointed. But that dismay is your problem, not theirs. They never said that they were right all of the time and probably never even asked for the role of being your advisor, you picked them so don't complain. Hopefully they gained as much as you did in the process.

My dad often said that he would never have tried to train anyone else except me. I have also said there was no one else in the world who could have taken the training, given the only way that he could deliver it. We were like two meteors in the universe, able to run concurrently for a while but destined to veer apart. But that time together was precious for us both and probably valued differently, but nonetheless was pivotal in both our development as businessmen and as people. Mentors give us what they are capable of which often does not include saying that we are good, or they are proud of what we accomplished. They are not perfect, for if they were they would not need us and we would never have the chance to travel along side them in space for the short time that we can.

Chapter 21

I love people who tell me no. When people say that I am crazy or my ideas will never work I know I am on the right track. You are responsible for yourself for the good and the bad, you might as well be "in charge" of yourself and decide your own direction.

Catie the Lefty

5/28/2002

I had a rather unusual childhood growing up in Northern New Jersey. While most of my friends were concerned with football and baseball, my main sport activities centered on hunting and fishing. This was not all that strange since those were the sports my Dad liked.

When I first started to target shoot, it became apparent to my Dad that I had a problem. It seemed that although I was right handed I had a left master eye. This simply meant that my left eye dominated my right so when I lined up on anything, my left side had the "true" picture of what was happening. I thought this was a catastrophe until my Dad made the simple declaration that I had to learn to shoot lefty.

Since I loved to target shoot, and was not willing to give it up, I switched my gun to my other side and quickly learned to become a very good shot.

About six months ago I developed extreme tendonitis in my right arm. I normally play tennis at least four times a week year round and it constitutes a major portion of my weekly workouts. I did not want to give it up but the pain became so bad that I had to consider it until one morning I woke up and realized I had another elbow.

With that in mind I told my tennis coach I was going to learn to play from the left side. He thought I as crazy, as did most everyone else and I could not have done it on my own, but with his help I have developed into a decent lefty player. Again having a dominant left eye has helped in the transition. The rest afforded to my right arm, combined with a cortisone shot, has brought my right elbow pain level way down and enabled me to begin playing on that side again. But since lefty is so much fun, combined with the fact that people can't believe I can do it, I now play about equal time on both sides.

I am a coach for my daughter's softball team and we have a player named Catie. Although she loves the game, she could never hit the ball. She was always under or over it and was continually growing more frustrated every time she was at bat. Last week, I told her we were going to try an experiment and I explained to her about left master eyes and that I wanted her try to hit from the left side. She was skeptical but I found out today, that she had a few hits in the last game, which I missed.

In today's game she got more hits and has gone from a highly frustrated ball player to a slightly less frustrated twelve year old girl and one who can at least hit a softball, not a miracle but a nice step forward in a short amount of time.

We live our lives filled with labels. She is a righty, he is a lefty. He is good in sports, she is good in math. He is successful, she is brilliant. The negative labels do not mean anything bad unless they hold you back and the good labels don't mean anything positive either unless they spur you on to greater things. In my case the negative labels even mean positive things because I tend to try much harder when people say I can't do something.

I will never be a great left handed tennis player, but it does mean I can keep playing the sport I love as long as I have the option of playing from the other side. Catie will probably never be a major league softball player but it will be one more place when she can excel and it will only be from the opposite side.

Be careful when you tell someone that something can't be done, unfortunately most people will listen to you and give up, but there will be an occasional individual who will do everything to prove you wrong and probably make you look really bad for trying to stop them. Most people only say it can't be done because they don't have the confidence, backbone or ability to do it themselves; I love people like that because I get the double pleasure of proving them wrong and, hopefully, stopping them from doing it to someone else.

Do you make enough money to live in your dream location?

Chapter 22

Again, the way your life goes is up to you. Advice from others is helpful but only if it positively leads you forward.

Hebrew With a Western Accent

5/6/2002

I have always been interested in conservation and the ecology. About twenty-five years ago, during one of the numerous energy shortages in our country, I decided to do something about it and helped create the *New Jersey Gasohol Association*. Our mission was a simple one which was to promote the use of grain based alcohol as an additive to extend existing gasoline supplies. At the same time it would also give our domestic farmers another outlet for their crops and reduce our dependence on fossil fuels.

The idea started to gain momentum and since I was already an aid to the State Assistant Assembly Minority leader it was relatively easy to get his endorsement. The first time he came to speak to our group I had invited my parents. My Dad, who was also my boss was therefore in the audience and while I was getting ready to speak I noticed him writing something down. It turned out he had been writing notes, critiquing my performance. When the shortage eased up, interest in our idea died and our country lost another chance to help ourselves become less dependent on others for energy.

It was now twenty-five years later and I was at my Temple. I belong to a Minyan group, which meets on Saturday mornings. We run the services ourselves and our members include a few rabbis as well as a Hebrew teacher. Since I am neither, it can get a little intimidating when I am leading the service, reading parts in Hebrew and knowing that they understand the language fluently and I don't.

I learned how to read Hebrew for my Bar Mitzvah some thirty-three years ago and over time I have gotten a little rusty with some of pronunciations. People who were fluent would say I had a "western" accent when it came to reading, a kind way to say I had added a few quirks to the language to make it my own.

The Hebrew Teacher in our group offered to write down a few helpful hints to rid me of my "accent" and I readily thanked her, wanting to be as close to perfect as possible. Last week, while I was leading I saw her writing down notes as I was speaking. As time went on I watched her write more notes and I was suddenly taken back in time seeing my father do the same thing at the Gasohol meeting.

I could feel my power seeping from my body, she would write something down and I would feel worse and stumble and I knew I had to do something. Then I got an idea, I stopped the service and told everyone what a wonderful thing the teacher was doing for me by writing down my mistakes. The only problem,

I said, was that she was doing most of her writing while I was speaking English which was starting to throw me off because she was now correcting me in two languages!

I got my intended result, which was laughter from the congregation, the teacher said she was writing when I was talking in English because that is when she had the time and I was immediately back in control of the situation.

By identifying what was going on and my loss of power I was able to see a way to stabilize the situation and make it work for me. The congregation was impressed that I wanted to get better and happy I cared enough to do it. The Hebrew teacher loved the attention that she got as being the "expert" and was also happy to be shown giving me support. By bringing the situation out in the open everyone got a plus.

Selling is the exchange of goods and services between two people or groups. But in order for that exchange to go the way that you want, you must be in control. It does not have to look like you are in command as long as you know you are and can steer the events as you choose.

The best selling is where everyone wins. In this case I got help with my Hebrew and held command, the Hebrew teacher was acknowledged as an expert and offered thanks for helping me by the group and everyone, as a whole, felt great because it's members were taking an extra effort to make things go better and working together.

Nothing is by accident, and even when it seems that luck has taken over, often instead it is a very smart salesman (insert any name you want, politician, owner, manager) who has viewed the options and decided what was in everyone's best interest.

You can leave your fate in the hands of others like me, who will gladly make the decisions for you, or you can guide your own life and events yourself, either way the decision will be made and life will go on. Your chances of getting what you want will usually be better if you guide your own destiny but you can't help to put yourself into position if you can't read the playing field and the players operating on it.

Chapter 23

Sometimes living with a salesman (i.e. crazyman) for a father has its drawbacks.

Gloves For a Calmer Mind

4/16/2001

My family and I were in Washington for a long weekend to go to a Bat Mitzvah. We were there with my sister-in-law and her family. Like us, they also have a teenage son. The first night we got there we were all tired except for my fourteen and their sixteen-year-old and they wanted to go out for coffee. Actually, they just wanted to go out but the grown-ups were all a little worried about them being out in a strange area at night.

Before they left, (and yes, they had a cell phone and explicit instructions to be back within the hour) I asked my son if he had gloves, as it was a cold night. He said no that he did not need them and I said he had to take mine. When he asked why, I passed by the part that his hands would get cold and I wanted him to be comfortable. I went to the main reason which was that if someone attacked him and he got into a fight, which has never happened, then he might need to hit someone with his fists, he is martial arts trained. If he hits someone and has skin to skin contact, I know from my martial arts training, the odds are good that blood will exchange from his attacker to him. When blood is exchanged there is a high probability that diseases can also be transmitted.

Far fetched you might think? I don't agree because professional boxing has banned HIV fighters for the exact reason I mentioned.

My son looked at me like I was from Mars but he took the gloves and went on his way. Another example in his mind of his Dad's incredible ability to be paranoid. On the contrary, I think it was another example of thinking ahead and not having to worry about something because you were prepared.

All of our customers are thinking about reducing their vendor pools in an attempt to be more efficient and economical. One of them approached us to become their major worldwide supplier. In order to accomplish this we undertook a complete review of their operations, to put together a plan which we think takes into account all of their concerns and fears and approach it from a viewpoint that will benefit all.

Our whole effort is based on giving them what they want, more security for their product flow, better tracking, faster deliveries, saving money through better prices and higher efficiency and most importantly making sure that their assembly lines never go down and they always have the correct products to use.

Just like being prepared with the gloves we are trying to look ahead to see what possible events could occur and deal with them first so they become pluses for us and we win the top spot. Selling is all preparation which has to extend throughout your entire being. You cannot be careless in some areas and careful in others. The big leagues of selling, where millions of dollars are at stake, always attract the best. You are fighting against people who will do virtually anything for the business, and you stand out only if you are ready for what has not yet happened.

I have never had to use my gloves for a fight, but there have been situations where, besides being cold, I have been very glad I had them. They have given me that extra bit of confidence to know I do not have to hold back if I do happen to get into a problem. Because in a fight, like in business, you don't want to be thinking of negative possibilities when you are in the midst of action. You have to be able to act with a clear head and not have a worry that could slow your reaction time.

In life, as in sales, stuff happens. If you are prepared for everything you can think of then you can afford to concentrate on what is happening at that moment, a luxury unavailable to many.

Would you be in your dream location alone?

Are you alone now?

Chapter 24

Whenever I think of my past I often center on what I did wrong. This is probably the reason why I try to live in the present or dream about the future. You can't hide from your past deeds so you might as well learn to accept yourself for what you are, capitalize on your strengths, reduce your weaknesses and excel at what you can be.

Your Past Is Your Greatest Asset

6/6/2002

I was away for a few days of cross-country skiing in the Massachusetts Berkshires with my family. As it turned out there wasn't enough snow, therefore when we arrived I went out for a walk in the late afternoon. To get ready for the walk I put on my cotton socks, woolen socks, pants, boots, outer pants, 3 shirts, a jacket that could zip up the front so I could let the warm air out when I got too hot and my cell phone. I figured I did not need my laptop. I had goggles for my eyes and full-face protection made of felt that went down to my shoulders. As I walked out the door I told my family that, knowing how I looked they could pretend they did not know me, something I am sure they had done before, I would take no offense.

The wind chill was below zero and it was starting to get dark as I went into the forest. I love the woods, and in this case, according to the tracks in the snow I was the first human to set foot in there for some time. The snow showed that one or two horses had been through, some mice and rabbits. I learned to track animals from my Dad, he also taught me how to dress for the woods while growing up fishing and hunting.

He taught me how to be able to handle myself alone, to know what direction I was going and how to get back from where I was. He also taught me how to read the sky, know what types of weather could be coming, all about the various trees, flowers and rocks and how to enjoy myself in the face of weather conditions that others would think unforgiving.

What he taught me was how to prepare for what I was going into so that I did not have to focus on personal well being or harm and could enjoy what the surroundings had to offer. It got to the point where having everything I needed, because I prepared correctly, was actually a point of pride and enjoyment. The same thing goes for the outdoors in the summer when it was 90 degrees and above. I am out there in long sleeves, pants and a hat knowing how the sun will directly react on my skin and also knowing my limits as to how much water to bring and how far I can push myself.

When I was about five years old I used to walk with my toes pointed out. It affected my ability to run and after consulting with a doctor my Dad got a piece of 2 x 4 lumber and instructed me to lay it on our driveway and learn to walk across it. Obviously, as soon as I could walk across that plank, my feet would be straight and my problem would be solved. I knew its purpose and I also knew how impossible it was for a five year old, especially this one, to do it. I tried and

NOTES

kept trying and the frustration built up in me until I cried out in anguish and the tears seemed to flow forever. I could not do it, time after time, I failed and cried. But, slowly I started to be able to make the journey.

The ability to run was paramount to every physical venue that I wanted to pursue, of which my Dad was aware. I could literally not run until I learned to walk again. He later told me that hearing me cry was heart breaking but he knew, for my own good, I had to do it. While I was never Olympic caliber in any sport I am now good in some, better in others and the rest we will not mention.

Preparation is everything and without it you can never get into the big leagues where the real money is made. You must have the basics before you can get onto the playing field and that goes for sports, school, work and life.

My salesmen look at me and I know they think they can do the same things I can. The only problem is that I have been training for the job since birth. They have only been seriously training for selling since they began working for us. They cannot even understand the playing field until they rack up some life experience in their jobs.

Good salesmen are not born, they are all made from having the basic good ingredients and then using life experience to mold those attributes to whatever form they best fit. You have no right to expect of yourself, and no one else does either, that you should immediately know what to do to sell. Your willingness to step out and try to sell in the first place puts you into a category that few people would ever dare enter. The only problem is that those who fear the game are in it anyway they just don't realize it.

Any contact between two people is a selling situation. Pretending it is not predetermines that you can never optimize your level of success.

Your life experience is your selling experience; you just have to know how to analyze it to get the needed information. You don't need sales school and you don't need to spend a fortune to be trained. You just need a roadmap of your life to be able to think back and figure out what you were selling, to whom and when and if you were successful. After that you can use what seemed to work successfully and try it out for a while and see if it fits, if it does then use it, if not try something else.

As we say, the concept is simple but not easy. It means to view your life from a different perspective, and that brings us right back to the 6 rules of selling which are you keys to determine where you have been, where you are and how far you are going. Check out the rules and sit down in a quiet place, pick an event in your life and analyze it from the perspective of those rules and you will probably be surprised as to what actually happened as opposed to what you thought happened. Don't waste your best asset, which is you, because if you to say no to your past then you are destined to live the same mistakes again.

Rule #1

Selling is the exchange of goods and services between one person and another.

Rule #2

You can never get what you want from someone else until you define first what they want and then satisfy their need. Only then will you have a chance of getting what you want in return.

Rule #3

The most important thing to anybody, apart from their family, is their job. The 2nd most important thing is a better job.

Rule # 4

You are there to do business never let your emotions get in the way of closing a deal.

Rule #5

If you are not prepared to put your life on the line then you will be beaten by someone who will.

Rule #6

Failure is not weakness.

Chapter 25

Democrat or Republican, liberal or conservative, structure equals success no matter what direction you come from.

Regine

8/18/2000

I met a woman named Regine on a flight from New Hampshire to New Jersey. Actually I had been dropped off in front of the airport and was heading the wrong way towards the parking area, my sense of direction has never been that good, and she was nice enough to point me in the right way.

It turned out that we were both going to the same airport in New Jersey, on the same flight so we took turns in the waiting room watching each others bags while we each went on errands and then settled down to chat.

I quickly learned that she was a mother of two, divorced, very successful and driven which was very evident by the two power beams emitting from her head masquerading as blue eyes. I almost never notice anyone's eyes but hers were an immediate guide to her personality, which was quick, intelligent, aggressive and nice.

You could tell immediately that she was strong willed and determined to meet the world on her own terms and by the looks of her, the world was giving in. But she had more then that, she had a plan, a set of goals for her and her two children and was not counting on anyone else in the world to help her.

She had laid out her life to insure that she had the time to spend with her children and for herself and while work was very important, it had its place. In order to insure the survival of her dreams she had developed a structure that would not only defend and support them but would increase her ability to meet life on her terms.

What a wonderful thing structure is. To many people it is a straight jacket of conformity that envelops them like a constricting snake, they can't breathe and they gasp for the life of impulsiveness. But the truth is there can be no life advancement without having the blueprint to nurture and promote it.

Structure is not something to be loathed, it is something to be embraced and revered. Knowing that certain things are expected, demanded, required and longed for helps to give our lives an order to a chaotic world. It enables us to know what we have to do in order to get the results we want.

Being successful=get in early, work hard and use your head.

Have a healthy body=good food, positive thought and a good life style

Equations are great and cannot be ignored. The law of Newton is correct: for every action there is an equal and opposite reaction. In the cause of having structure, you are in charge of the action and reaction. If you leave life to impulse then the reaction is out of your hands and your life is left to the plans of others.

When you think of a planner what comes to your mind? Someone who thinks ahead, is ready for all possible situations, enjoys being able to go through and triumph in tough situations? In other words someone you want to have around especially in hard times. Being ready for life is not a sign of being dull and uninteresting, on the contrary, being prepared is the sign of someone who is ready to take on the world on their terms, pay the consequences and reap the rewards for their actions.

The responsibility for your life is yours whether you take it on directly or not. Generally the more you plan and the more structure that you have, the more you can fully utilize your resources and efficiency and the more successful you will become in any area.

I like my life because:

Chapter 26

Just because you don't see the direction I am headed, do not assume I am wrong.

I Will Back Up My Son

12/31/2001

I had an incredible idea the other day, it was going to revolutionize how to get sales on a massive basis, which would allow me to cross pollinate across vast stretches of the American Manufacturing and Service sectors. Incredibly excited, I wrote down the idea and started to circulate it amongst my closest compatriots to get their reactions. For although I will go ahead with an idea even if I get no outside support, in fact I will sometimes go with a new idea specifically because everyone else thinks it is a crazy idea, in this case I was actually looking for positive feedback.

I sent the idea to one of my friends, I followed up, after not hearing from a him a few hours later.

He said he had read the idea, proceeded to not only prove he had not read the whole thing, but then even lambasted it without giving it a second thought. This offhanded treatment of my "great" idea sent me into a rage and it was all I could do to contain myself when I politely suggested he go back and read the whole thing so he could discuss it intelligently. The next day he called to say he did not think it was a good idea but he really did not understand it anyway. He then said that he had the greatest idea about how to sell and market and he sent me his "stuff" and wanted my reaction to it right away.

My first inclination was to tell him his idea was lousy because he trashed my mine without a fair trial but I read it and even though I did not think a lot of it I tried to give him some positive feedback. I also told him that he had missed out on being part of my new plan, which did not upset him. So he went his way and I am going mine, neither of us wanting a part of the other's, but I least I did not try to destroy his idea before it was tested.

My son Ben wants to be a rock musician, that is his dream and his passion. He is also an honor student, fair, trustworthy, honest and one of the greatest people I have ever met even though he is only fifteen years old. I know what passion is like and I know what a "fire in the belly" can feel like when you set your sights on a goal that almost everyone thinks is impossible.

Of my three children, Ben, my oldest, would seem to have the best chance of coming into our family business, learning what is needed, and plugging in his passion and brains to take our company to the next level. Also, knowing what passion is, I would never tell him his dream of being a rock star is impossible. They said the same thing for anyone going into sales, the chance to make big money almost never happens so why even bother to try? The answer, of course is that someone will make it, and if the person deserves to make it big then it will happen.

I know that Ben has to give his music a fair try, for whatever years it takes, and if he isn't as successful then, he will look to re-direct his passion somewhere else and I hope that target is my company. But first he has to try things his way and I have to be 100% behind him in order for him to have the optimum chance of success and if not, no regrets about not having achieved his first dream.

Although he is only fifteen I respect his passion and belief in himself as much as I respect that in me. I also knows how it feels when someone else tries to trash your dreams because they have either not made it themselves, are jealous about your ability or want to showcase their own above the ideas of others.

Your chances of success in this world are greatly reduced if you have no dreams of your own which can supercharge your energy and imagination to propel you to where you have a chance of success. No dreams does not mean you are doomed to failure, only that you need to find someone with a passion whose outcome you want to be a part of and partner with them. The passion and the energy allows you the energy to see what others can't and push the borders of what people think is possible. They allow you the portal to go from normal to abnormal in all directions and give you the chance to become something that few others can achieve.

But being a part of the group who tries to undermine those with a vision or negates their possibilities or worse yet tries to slow down their progress will be doomed to a life of negativity, depression and a direct path to eventual failure. If you do not see where someone is headed do not assume they don't know what they are doing. Focus on your own limitations and try and figure out why the other people are getting to their finish line first. Remember it is always easier to say it can't be done, but it is so much more profitable and satisfying to prove that it can.

Chapter 27

Don't tell me how to spell my own name!

The Bagel Store

10/19/2000

I was minding my own business, like always, when my beautiful wife asked me to pick-up some food at the bagel store the day before Yom Kippur, the Jewish Day of Atonement. Now I don't know about you, but after I fast for a day I can get pretty hungry, so it is really important to make sure the food is ready the second we declare that the fast is over. To accomplish this we had to get the food during the day before the fast started at sundown.

The only problem is that everyone else had the same idea and wanted to make sure that they also got there in time. My wife had determined that the food had to come from a particular store, she felt it is the best. Unfortunately, so did a majority of the rest of the Jewish world so the lines can be unbelievable.

Therefore, in order for me to not wait for an hour or more, I had to get there when it opened which this year meant 6:00AM on Sunday morning. Now granted, I usually like to sleep a little later on a Sunday morning but it was not an undue hardship to get up at 5:00AM so I could be finished by 6:30 and go walk with my friend in the woods as we do most Sunday mornings.

I got to the bagel store at 5:40AM and lo and behold it was open early. I raced into the store and there was one man ahead of me, and what a coincidence, he was an old friend of the family that I had known my whole life.

The woman behind the counter, Margie, whom I have known slightly for the past twenty years, we went to the same High School together, could not find my order. I repeated my last name and finally she found my food, looked at me, and said that I gave her the wrong last name and that was why she could not find it.

Now, how many times in your life have you had someone say that you gave them the wrong information when you know darn well you said it correctly? The problem was not your delivery of the information but their mis-hearing it. In any case it is never their fault. But in this case I even had a witness who reiterated that I had given my own last name correctly, which of course I did, but I had neither the time nor desire for an argument and that was the end of it.

Of course it left me with the impression of her incompetence but it reminded me of something much bigger. Most people, when in doubt or worried about something, will blame someone else as opposed to saying that they made a mistake because they weren't listening, did not understand or just messed up.

My father always taught me that the fastest way to diffuse a tense situation was admit that you made a mistake, that you would fix it right away and you were sorry. People are usually surprised that you will say that everyone makes mistakes and forgive you. In fact the act of forgiveness often lets them feel good about themselves so you, in a strange twist of fate, have almost done something nice for them. If you admit responsibility then most people will bend over backwards to help you to fix the problem. I have found that the truth really does set you free. You can admit something went wrong and then you are also able to take the credit when you do something correctly.

Stringently proclaiming your innocence or trying to blame someone else will almost unilaterally backfire on you whether it was your fault of not. If you screw up, and we all do, admit it, fix it, learn from it if possible and move on, don't make matters worse by not owning up to your actions.

I would make the following changes to my life:

I haven't made the desired changes to my life because:

Chapter 28

It is so simple: concentrate on who you are talking to and say what you mean.

To Alex

3/17/2001

My middle son Alex turned to me last night and asked me why there were so many jokes about Polish people. He innocently asked me if they were inherently dumber or did more stupid things than most people. I looked at him and asked him why there are so many jokes about Jewish people (we are Jewish) are we more stupid or more crazed about money than other groups? I saw the light bulb go off in his head, he had gotten the point and I did not have to go any further.

People say and do things that place limits on themselves all of the time and never realize it. I had a customer who kept referring to be "Jewed down" on various projects. Finally I said to him that I was Jewish. He said that he knew that and what was my point. He had never connected "Jewing down" with my religion. He never thought about what it meant and that someone Jewish could despise him for using that word.

This is not a piece on political correctness, it is about not taking anything for granted especially when dealing with other people. When in a selling situation, and since every interaction is a selling situation, you cannot put yourself on automatic. You always have to think about what you are saying, who is hearing it and who might hear about it again. Yes it means you always have to be careful, especially depending on how successful you want to be.

This also means you can never relax and just talk, because talk is what hurts people the most, and saying you don't mean something just means you told the truth and got caught doing it. Some people can feel what you are saying and others just take you literally, in any case you are responsible for whatever comes out of your mouth. It doesn't matter if you are tired, cold, hungry, angry, drunk, high or trying to get what you want, the responsibility always is and will remain yours.

Knowing that gives you an immense amount of power when dealing with others. By understanding this truth, where most people don't you can actually tell what they are really thinking by what they say. Often their words mask their real feelings but there is a code to everyone and if you concentrate and are around them often enough then you can unlock what they really are saying even if they are not conscious of it.

Selling and marketing yourself is an incredibly complex thing because things happen so fast that your mind can often not take in all of the variables before it is time for you to speak again. You have to be able to quicken your mind and force yourself to think more clearly and faster. My Dad was a champion at this. He had an very keen and quick mind which could take in incredible amounts of data, process them, and then capitalize on them. He used to continually speak faster around me when I first started to quicken my mind and sharpen my senses. It is an exercise I continue to this day because the faster and clearer I can think the more successful I become.

To be able to listen and process with increasing speed is a talent that can be learned an improved and you can start immediately. Concentrate on the person you are talking to, look at their eyes watch their faces see how they are conducting themselves and make mental notes. Listen to how they speak as well as what they say and that extra concentration will send you on your way to being able to move faster to get what you want.

The rewards in life go to those who deserve them, most of the time it is those people who can manipulate others around them for the good of everyone, you can't hope to do that if you can't keep up with the information coming in, all it takes is concentration and lots of practice.

I like my boss because:

Chapter 29

Accepting what you can't change does not mean you can't modify it.

Don't Settle—Exercise

1/7/2001

There are times in everyone's life when the stress of various events become more than at others. Some people smoke, others drink or fool around, I exercise.

Exercise is an amazing activity. Three days a week I work out in the gym in my office, I am always alone, first because it is usually 6:00 in the morning and secondly because no one else uses it. I usually spend about hour and forty-five minutes there which is usually enough time to sweat out the toxins in my body and just as importantly the demons in my mind.

I don't think most people give themselves the time to get rid of those bad things in their bodies, minds and spirits. Exercise is not just a losing of calories but a burning of the negative thoughts that permeate our minds if we don't exorcise them. And don't give me the "I don't have time excuse." If you sleep more than 7 ½ hours then you have time to exercise.

The other two work days of the business week I usually play tennis against my coach, one of whose joys in life is watching me run like a nut for balls I have no chance in getting. I have heard it rumored that some coaches actually let their student win a few points to keep them involved in the game. No such worry from my guy, he gets great happiness from trying to make sure I don't get anything that I don't earn. Therefore I can get extreme pleasure from making the occasional winner. But he and I know each other well and he understands that I rarely play percentage tennis, even though it would mean I would beat most of the people I play. He realizes that I am not out there to win, and in exchange for me not blaming him because I can't beat everyone he does not try and stop me from trying to kill the ball. Why do I often hit the ball as hard as I can? Again to get rid of the negative feelings in my body and it is fun, besides it is not my day job and therefore it doesn't count.

So much of what we have to do as parents, workers and in our lives is not fun, we should all try to maximize the pleasures we get when we can. My life has been particularly stressful lately. My company is expanding and we are moving to a new manufacturing facility that is triple our current space and costs about three times as much. I am hiring more people and spending money on equipment. This is all happening while the economy seems to be moving downward and the general feeling is that I am crazy for making the move and getting bigger now.

I knew this would be coming, I thought the economy would cool off and I knew that many people would not view our move as the most prudent of actions. Going against the general flow is always a difficult thing to do, human beings like to be parts of groups moving in the same direction, the problem with that is that the big money never flows toward them. It is in that counter position that

I am most comfortable because that has been where I have had my greatest successes and failures. The odds are optimized because the stakes are much bigger, I have committed my company and all its resources to this move and there is no turning back now.

I exercise therefore to keep my nervous energy somewhat in check so I can at least sit at my desk. I work out so I do not (often) go nuts toward my people, suppliers and customers. I exercise because it also enables me to harness that energy to positive things like working harder, smarter and longer as I need it. It is like having your own personal power generator that you can call on when you are tired, all you have to do is exercise and it produces. I know it seems crazy but if you can make yourself exercise when you are dragging then you will often get a burst of energy. Exercise will also allow you to act in a more humane way and let you separate the emotion from the reality and see how things really are.

It almost sounds like it is a drug and in a way it is. To not exercise would drive me crazy and irrational which is why I keep doing it, besides of course liking it.

Unfortunately like any drug the more you do the less it does so I have to keep increasing my workouts in duration, timing and intensity and it is having some effects. The first is that my body is in the best shape of my life and I am heartened when I look in the mirror. The more I exercise the more stress I can take which is good because that is only going to increase as time and the new move approaches. It also enables me to eat more and some types of food I do not normally let myself enjoy.

The bad side is that I am working out more than seven times a week, which takes a good amount of time, but of course my mind is working through most of that so I am still productive. Unfortunately a 44 year old body is probably not built to take as much punishment as I am giving so I ache a lot of the time.

As I write this it is a beautiful Sunday afternoon and I have worked out twice this morning, my normal for a Sunday. I want to be outside so I will probably try and force myself to take a walk. I know that once I am out there I will probably be fine and enjoy it, besides it will help to insure that I can sleep tonight and not stay up because I am worried.

You cannot get rid of the stresses you live under; you can only deal with them. Whichever path you choose will have good and bad things emanating from it. Using artificial means to deal with the stress and worry, like alcohol and drugs, are a mask of what is really happening. The best way to take on what is bothering you is head on and the best way to do it rationally is through the use of exercise that will not only help your mind, but also your body and soul.

Which is better, to have an aching body because you are pushing yourself to optimize your capability and deal with the matters at hand or settling for the decision that nothing more can be done anyway? I would trade a few aches and pains for more peace of mind any day.

Chapter 30

Unfortunately or fortunately, none of us are unique. It is simply a matter of how we handle life's choices that set us apart.

The Commuting Worm

6/28/2002

Part of my workouts during the week include a forty minute walk after I have finished in the gym. It is a grand part of my day, I get to be outside all year round, listen to the birds, watch the squirrels and let my mind wonder about everything.

A few days ago, after it had been raining, I noticed a big worm trying to pass over the sidewalk in front of me. Although I am germ phobic, I did have my trusty handkerchief with me and I helped the worm get to the other side into the grass.

A few days later I came across the same spot and that same worm was trying to go back the other way, once again across the sidewalk. Again I had my handkerchief and helped him along his way. This got me to thinking about why the worm would go to all that effort, first to cross the great divide and get cement burns on his stomach and then do it all over again a few days later.

Perhaps, I thought, his girlfriend lived on the other side of the walk which would have easily explained his perseverance in crossing. But why would he risk death to come back. Unless of course his job was on the other side and he had no choice. So there you have it, the first commuting worm and he probably never would have made it, if it had not been for me.

What would have happened if I had not come along, what would he have done? Like everything else in life it all comes down to basic needs. The worm wanted to see his girlfriend but still had to make a living so he had to make the dangerous commute which could have cost him his life, but he still did it, every day. Sounds pretty similar to what we do.

We spend our lives making life changing decisions which to others would seem crazy. What if a bird came by, instead of me when the worm was crossing, it would have been an instant snack. But we nevertheless feel that when we make these types of decisions, they do not seem so crazy, in fact they seem like intelligent rational courses of action.

When you think about it, is there any sanity to going to war? Two sides line up and blow each other apart, it seems crazy to anyone not directly involved but the only solution to those immersed in it.

Being in sales (read that *"life"*), as we all are, gives us a panoramic view of the world and a telescopic view of many of its individuals. We see people all the time seemingly not acting in their best interest, but they keep on doing the same thing all of their lives. How much wealthier and happier could they be if they just stepped back and thought about what they were doing and how it could be going better?

How much sense is their in commuting four hours a day to a job in the city, unless the quality of life for your family is at stake? How smart is it to smoke cigarettes when you know it will kill you? How easy is it to keep going when everyone says you are dead wrong about something but you keep trying?

There is nothing wrong with going against the flow and there is everything right in committing yourself in mind, body and soul to what you believe in but there is no law that says you have to do it in the toughest way possible. It is okay to make the journey pleasant, to have fun and remember that your life is yours to spend as you will. Every once in a while it is a good thing for us all to step back and watch ourselves. Are we where we want to be, concentrating on limited resources on the places we have chosen-or scratching our stomachs on cement in a futile attempt to cross a great divide, to get somewhere not in our best interest?

Which reminds me, I think the worm would have a lot easier time if he picked someone to date from his own side of the tracks or sidewalk, but then again it is not my decision and maybe he is enjoying the adventure of the journey as much as the fruits of his labors.

I don't like my boss because:

Chapter 31

Never, ever, enter into an agreement figuring it can't happen.

Too Good a Deal

7/2/2001

Being a Dad means you are part father, part judge, part friend and part business partner. The last item came up with my eleven year old daughter about four months ago. She came to me and said she wanted a laptop and I of course said that an eleven years old does not need one and I was not buying it. She then asked that if she saved up half would I then pay the rest?

Now as a parent I love to see that my children are willing to work and toil to get the things they want, besides learning the art of negotiation. I liked that she was willing to work for what she wanted, a long range project for an eleven year old is a very good thing. Besides, how could a pre-teenaged girl, with no job ever hope to put together 500.00? So I felt pretty safe in supporting her plan feeling there was very little chance it would happen.

Four months later, after she had saved her birthday and holiday money, done innumerable extra chores and making deals in every area of our lives, she handed me the final 18 dollars and said she was ready to buy the laptop.

Somewhat stunned I said okay, after all a deal was a deal and together with my money we ordered a laptop over the telephone. A few weeks passed and it did not arrive and finally I checked the computer manufacturer, got the shipper information, ran a trace and found out it had already been delivered and someone had already signed for it!

Somebody else had my daughter's computer. I called my wife and read her the name on the receipt and it turned out to be a neighbor down the street. This seemed very weird and when the person finally got home that night we asked her about our package and she said the only computer she got was the one she had ordered.

It turned out we had both ordered computers from the same manufacturer that were both delivered on the same day, think of the chances of that! Also, she had not looked on the labels to see to whom they were addressed. The problem was that, after she unpacked her stuff, she had given the boxes to her brother to discard and never finished looking in them. Her brother, as it turned out, found my daughter's computer and decided it was a mistake by the manufacturer and that he had gotten a free laptop and was keeping it. By the time we found out who had it, he had been playing with it for a week.

I told the neighbor I wanted either for her to pay for another computer, after all who knew what her brother had done to my daughter's, or we would put a claim in with the shipper who had delivered it to the wrong address. My neighbor was great, apologized for what happened, brought me over a check and I ordered another laptop the next morning.

I find it amazing that her brother would think that a free laptop would not be missed, besides it being the wrong thing for him to keep it under false pretenses. In the end he had put his sister into a very awkward position since we all have to live together on the same street, he forced his own sister to buy my daughter a new one.

If something seems too good to be true, whether in business or at home, it usually is. No deal that is "too good" will ever last because one side will never hold to the deal. The best relationships are two sided where both sides gain with every interaction so the bond continues to get stronger as well as the level of trust. Going for a deal too good to be true may work once, maybe, but over the long haul you will get beaten because once someone knows what you are like, it is very easy to trap and manipulate you later for much bigger gains.

In this case our neighbor's brother "went for it" which resulted in him getting a computer but also resulted in extreme embarrassment for his sister and probably a large amount of distrust between the two of them which could effect them permanently. A laptop will be outdated in a few years but relationships between brother and sister, and neighbors for that matter, can go on for many years and it is silly, if not stupid to jeopardize it all for a quick kill.

I could do a better job than my boss because:

Chapter 32

Sometimes you have to step back before you can go forward.

Still a Kid

3/4/2002

When I was twelve years old I was overweight, self conscious, incredibly shy, seemed to have few friends and was afraid of almost everyone. Actually that wasn't all true, in retrospect I was chubby not fat, a decent athlete, had a bunch of friends and was a lot further advanced that I gave myself credit for. But the strength of my self perception was not going to be swayed by the reality of the rest of the world and my insecurity always seemed to be there no matter what the situation, except in one place.

I had one really good talent that had showed itself at an early age. I had started target shooting when I was five years old and by the time I was twelve was a competitive level skeet shooter. Skeet shooting is a sport for five people consisting of shooting clay saucers that are launched through the air from two standing stations. The target shooter moves to various positions where they would take turns trying to break as many "clay pigeons" as possible. I was really good at it and even better than that, I was usually the only "kid" shooting.

My Dad and I would go most weekends and although I entered the range a pre-teenager, by the time I came out, I was one of the guys. You see the people in the range did not care if I was twelve, overweight and not an athlete. Actually they may have preferred that I was and not as good a shot because it must have been tough for them, including my Dad, to be beaten week after week by a kid half their size. It was an amazing thing for me to be better at something than the adults and greater yet to be treated as an equal. This was the only place where I had respect from grown-ups and I reveled in it.

I also loved the time with my Dad and being on a somewhat equal basis. We shared the love for shooting and being out together for a few more years until I grew to love different things and he and I grew apart.

Later I went into the family printing business and my Dad attained the highest power position on earth which is the combination boss/father. We battled together as a team against the world for fun and profit and against each other jockeying for position and power. He fully retired a few years ago and went back to just being my Dad but the gap between us was still there and we both looked for ways to try and close it.

In every stage in life, whether it be between parent and child, siblings or deep commitments of any type, there needs to be something to bridge the two parties together where they can share a common ground so they can begin the next stage of their relationship. My Dad and I went shooting today, the first time in some years. The competition for business and power was now gone and it was time to go back to, not being a father and son like it used to be, but one of more equal footing on a basis of respect for past accomplishments and moving toward future goals.

It was like going back in a time warp, the range looked like the same, and the people although different in name, dressed, acted and looked as they had thirty years before. It was nice to share the time, and it was fun reliving some of the moments but it was really good just being together and it could only have happened in a "safe" place for the both of us. I have no urge to be a kid again, I love my life where it is, but returning to a place of safety means that the same magic has a chance to work again. That range is one of the few spots where we can both be the people that we are to each other to be and still be happy with ourselves at the same time. That place was a sanctuary for us both many years ago and hopefully there is a chance for the magic to work again.

I feel that I am where I should be at this point in my life because:

___

___

___

___

___

___

___

___

More education would help me because:

___

___

___

___

___

___

___

___

Memoirs of a Sales Warrior:

PART II

My Way

I warned you about reading this part of the book. Here is where the tough stuff begins- Boot Camp!

You want to learn how to sell?

You want to learn what you are made of?

Then read on and see what happened to me. If you think it was tough you were right, if you think it is still tough you are right again. It is time to start learning about yourself.

CHAPTER 33

Now It's Your Turn

6/16/2002

Now you get to have a lot of fun, because it is your turn. It is time for you to stop living your life as a random group of events and start to plan a structure of where you want to go.

The first thing you need to do is define who you are. That has to go across your whole life in terms of mind, body and soul. Here is a check-list to give you a place to start.

There are no right or wrong answers. Photocopy this list so that you can rate others.

Rate yourself below on a scale of 1-10 with 1 being least and 10 being most

ARE YOU:	*least* 1	2	3	4	5	6	7	8	9	*most* 10
Aggressive										
Great physical Beauty										
Great inner beauty										
Fat										
Thin										
Like to cook										
Neat										
Sloppy										
Healthy										
Sick										
Optimistic										
Pessimistic										
Happy										
Sad										
Dejected										
Update										
Poor										
Rich										
Have a Good job										
Have a Great job										
Have No job										
Want to be a business owner										

(continued)

ARE YOU:	least 1	2	3	4	5	6	7	8	9	most 10
Want kids										
Want to be married										
Want a boy/girlfriend										
Thirst for life										
Have a thirst for adventure										
Have a thirst for structure										
Disciplined										
Sarcastic										
Caustic										
Loving										
Caring										
Funny										
Thoughtful										
Provocative										
Smart										
Knowledgeable										
Want more education										
Want pets										
Satisfied										
Loves the journey										
Goals mean everything										
Constant motion										
Need sleep										
Need exercise										
Love to exercise										
Gambler										
Tolerant										
Like to think										
Like to invent										
Like to get along										
Try to get along										
Like to start trouble										
Like to dream										
Go after dreams										
Other people are good										

(continued)

ARE YOU:	least 1	2	3	4	5	6	7	8	9	most 10
Other people are happy										
The world is a good place										
The world is a bad place										
Make the world better										
Want kids										
Like to help										
Want to be left alone										
Hyper										
Calm										

After you have rated yourself, now rate the people closest to you, members of your family, your boss, people who work for you. Yes, it will take some work but we are talking about your life and future happiness so some effort may be required.

Now you have a good profile of everyone around you—are you satisfied with what you found? If not then perhaps it is time to make some changes. If you are trying to move ahead in all areas of your life you probably need to be surrounded by people who would not only like to see you get there and support you along the way but will also try and help you to make the journey easier and faster.

Hopefully you will like the answers you come up with, if not, you have some strong thinking to do. My advice is to surround yourself with positive individuals, who will not only accelerate your journey, but make it much more pleasant. Try to remember to have fun!

NOTES

Chapter 34

You never know your strengths until you are forced to seek them out, often under pressure. You will also probably be surprised at how good you are.

Golden Hands

12/11/2000

When I had just entered into the family printing business there were always lots of jobs that needed "hand finishing work". Whether it was collating, punching or hand cutting there was always a lot to do. Unfortunately, I felt that I had no talent in this area, I had never been good with my hands, in an artistic way so I keep avoiding doing it. My wonderful father never satisfied with anyone's refusal, especially mine, to try and do new things attacked the situation. He simply declared that I had "golden hands," those were his words. Therefore I, being the possessor of golden hands, by definition had to be competent at this type of work. Unbelievably enough since he believed it, I eventually did also. As time went on, I actually even became good at it, and as I watch my hands move now I have wonder for my father for being able to instill the confidence where none had been before.

If you have called our office, you probably have spoken to Peter; he is in charge of accounts payable and receivable areas. He has had almost no formal training in accounting, bookkeeping or computers but he runs those sections for us and is our in-house computer specialist. In fact last week, our computer network was hit with a virus, and you guessed it, Peter, along with our consultant on the phone, spent 14 hours and cleansed our systems.

We are putting in a new accounting/ full production system. Peter is putting in modifications that the software consultant is probably going to use with his other clients. My man is helping the consultant; I should be charging the Software Company, instead of the other way around.

Peter was the "kid" who a few years ago did not know how to use a computer and had no intention of learning how. This was the guy, who people looked at and said had limited potential. His success has been spectacular and I am very proud of him.

In my dating life of asking out hundreds of woman and I found out one truly amazing thing. If I thought a woman was beautiful and she didn't, then over time she could convince me that she wasn't.

In business I have learned some major lessons. The first is that I do not have to be a good artist, industrial designer, bookkeeper, and be able to fix computers. I have to have a basic knowledge of all areas but I can always hire specialists to do the actual work. I can hire people to do almost anything as long as I hire the right ones.

These "right" people do not have to be suitable for eternity or even a decade. They only have to be right for that moment in time for the purpose that I have now. Some people are perfect for a specific job and once it is done they begin to self-destruct and have to move on until they can find another "right" position.

Unfortunately, this is extremely costly for the boss who has to keep training people for those who have left. Therefore you are always trying to maximize the people you have and keep them as productive as possible for as long as you can and trying them in new areas.

This is what makes being an employer so frustrating and wonderful at the same time. It is like a game of chess moving people around to keep them and you happy. The rough times come when you have an employee who suddenly starts going into a decline. Something goes wrong for them at home or the office, there is an economic or emotional problem or all of the above and they lose their drive. You have to find a way to turn the tide, some way to resurrect them before they have deteriorated too far, not only because they are an employee but because you also care about them as people.

You feel frustrated because you think that if you were a better boss, or if you were smarter then you could keep all of your people perfectly motivated at 100% efficiency. But we are all human and many times people don't act as what we see as in their own best interest.

Maybe that is best because you are their boss, not a father or parent, not a god or deity. You are in charge trying to safeguard your own position, worth and the growth of your company. You are trying to fulfill the needs of your company and offering in exchange, a job which will create a temporary, happy way station for your employee after their last job and before their next.

Mostly, nothing is forever, look at the divorce rate, but once in a while, when the odds go in your favor you might be lucky enough to hook up with a spouse and an employee with whom you can spend the rest of your life. These situations are rare and you can't expect that it will ever happen.

The signs are easy to spot when "it" stops working. The employee doesn't smile as much, they look unhappy. They don't give 100% and the other team members notice immediately, especially in a small company, that the employee has begun to coast. For a short amount of time the other team members try to help, out of loyalty and friendship, but reality will kick in and then they want the less contributing member to be sacrificed for the good of the cause. The team is right to want this because they can never get the full rewards for their work if one member is holding them back.

You as boss notice the signs right away and informally talk to the employee but you know that they are on a path of no return. And you start gathering incidents that you can write down for a formal warning which means you are getting ready to fire them soon. It is a dance played out all too often. You, as the boss have to have the formal "talk" where the warning is given, your stomach is a mess because you hate the thought of someone self-destructing. Especially someone you have spent a fortune on training. Then you wait a few more weeks hoping for an improvement that will last more then a few days, which doesn't happen, and 99% of the time you realize that it is pointless. The very existence of the employee has become destructive to the wholeness of the company environment and you take action.

I run my company, like a family. It may sound hoaky but it is true. I treat my employees very well, the way I would want to be treated, I care about them and I like to think they care about me. But we all know that business is business and if they can't keep up then they have to go. The now ex-employee can take it easier someplace else. Maybe they make less money, have less fun, not have that surge of excitement about going after new markets that have never been tapped before, but they will also not be watched or pushed or instilled with as much responsibility as I do. Maybe they need a rest, but whatever the reason they have to move on and hopefully they can find their next situation quickly.

I have fired a fair amount of people in my working career. The ones that hurt the most are the people that I feel have the potential for great things and don't live up to them. Unfortunately for them, if I think they have great potential and they don't, like a beautiful woman over time they can convince me that they are right. But there are enough people out there who do not look the part, don't know their capabilities and just have to be shown that they have "golden hands" and they are the ones that I'm after.

NOTES

Chapter 35

Don't blame them for your giving up.

My Nose Is Not That Big

7/7/2001

My Sister and I went to the Same College-she was a senior and I was a freshman. I had broken my leg, stupidly playing football for fun. We were facing a football player in the aisle outside my dormitory room. He was a stupid man, all muscle, no brains, the kind that get into college because he can play a sport and he lived in the state. He had just looked at me and call me a "_____" Jew. My reaction was to hit him with my crutch. By the way, it bounced off him like a swizzle stick-but I hate bullies. After that we became friends, once you stood up to him he was fine.

When I was thirteen, I was a caddie at the golf course very near my house. The fact that it was a private club, which meant that no Jews, among other groups, were allowed did not bother me because it was close and I wanted a job. When one of the other caddies tried to steal the pretzels out of my back pocket I turned around and hit him. A fight later ensued, I won but lost the battle because everyone wanted to fight me and I left the job for safer territories.

I am a Jew; I am pushy, smart and am perfectly happy to work until I drop to get what I want. That is me and I know it.

When I was in Hong Kong, I was different in another way, I was a white Caucasian where being Jewish did not matter, but being taller than everyone else did. My non-likeness to everyone else was offset by my size, I had no problem, and my wife who is 4'10" did.

It matters whether you are Jewish, dull or a dumb football player, these are the traits that make us up and trying to ignore them or explain them away is a serious waste of our energy. The hardest thing a person can do is take stock of themselves and realize both the good and the bad areas.

It is easy to see the bad parts, because that is what gives us the excuses to fail or not go as far as we might. They say I am too short for basketball, I am not smart enough to make a million dollars a year, I am not good looking enough to get that girl.

When I was in college, I assessed the dating situation quickly; most of the other guys went home for the weekend or spent their time on studying or sports. I, and a few smart others realized that we had a bonanza on our hands with a multitude of woman with no one to take them out. It was an amazing environment and I took full advantage of it. There was no woman that I considered too good for me to ask out and I was always amazed at who said yes and who turned me down. Often the prettiest women never got to go anywhere because most guys were all too afraid to try.

I am not a Hollywood movie star in looks, but I have more than enough, combined with my aggressiveness to go after anyone, and did. This was fortunate because when I finally met my wife I had done everything I had wanted and was ready to settle down with a suitable, intelligent, wonderful woman and I could view her in that way.

We have no excuses for not being able to see ourselves clearly. Sure I have a nose that is bigger than some, yes I am losing my hair, yes my singing, which I do all the time, can be somewhat bothersome, but I know what I am capable of and that is what keeps me striving to get where I want to go.

Many people talk about hitting the wall, almost no one ever gets anywhere near it because they give up with things get tough.

We have to all stop thinking about what we can't do, because that is easy, and begin to focus more on where we can go. Even in an economic environment like we have now, especially in that type of confusion, the options are infinite for those daring enough to step up to their own personal wall, spit at it and jump over.

Failing is easy, knowing what is wrong is simple. Going for the brass ring is the tough part, and focusing on what can be done at all times is what can change a bigoted in-state football player into someone who can actually be friends with a Jew.

I don't have the level of education that would help me because:

____

____

____

____

____

____

____

____

____

____

____

____

____

CHAPTER 36

It was a great idea, it just took a lot of years for everyone to realize it.

Nothing Speaks Louder Than Showing Up

10/30/2000

Trying to market yourself, your ideas and your business should be easy today. Make a website, throw it up on an internet server, and within a few days and millions of hits later, you have the dream job of your life, your company has enough business to go public and you are eyeing your first vacation condo in Italy! Unfortunately, it doesn't work that way now, and it never worked that way before.

With the advent of each new type of medium like radio, television, computers, home computers and today the Internet, each new technology jump seemed to sound the death knell for the need to personally market ourselves and our companies. But the truth is there are no technological innovations that can do away with the need to be able to market and sell ourselves "belly-to-belly."

It is the ability to understand, utilize and manipulate each new medium that enables some of us to be able to achieve our dreams, or least a percentage of them, in all areas of life.

About seven years ago, when marketing on the Internet was just starting to take shape, I got the idea to put together a number of companies into a consortium to create a reliable virtual full service and product supermarket. As a group all "under one website," we were going to offer added value to our existing customers by making it more convenient to buy from us and providing the credibility that came from being associated with each other. Participants would all cross-market in return for a 5% commission for referring sales to each other. I thought the 5% commission would be enough incentive to loosen people up about sharing their contacts and we could all cross-pollinate sales for each other and grow our businesses in unison.

Great idea, right? I got a bunch of companies together and started mass advertising through the web. The problem was that by relying on web sales, we had to rely on people browsing the Internet and at that point in time there was not a lot of traffic. Therefore we did not have a large group to advertise to and the result was no hits and no sales. The idea was good—as proven by many similar websites that came into being during the recent "dot.com" craze. Unfortunately, seven years ago we couldn't generate enough interest to create the percentages necessary to get sales. The idea died within 6 months.

Within the following year, our company, Ideal Jacobs, was one of the first to try to market on the Internet. Those were the heady days when you could still get a great name with ".com" after it and most people still had no idea what the Internet was, let alone what it might be able to do. After various attempts at increasing our online marketing and sales and trying to create stronger relationships with our customers via e-mail and over the internet, we failed to achieve marketing Nirvana.

And then reality finally set in. There was nothing we were doing with our website that brought new or greater value to our customers. We established a nice, clean, informative site and used it as a holding area for new product announcements and company developments. It was a place where our customers and prospective customers could go to check on us and see what was happening. We updated it occasionally but never really gave it a lot of thought or work.

Just having a website means nothing. Even getting random hits means nothing. Only those hits that translate into inquires and sales can mean something and the vehicle for that can be a website, newspaper or radio advertising, telemarketing, direct selling, carrier pigeon, pack mule, etc. In fact, when I was just starting out my father did not bother with formal advertising at all. He pointed to the door and told me to go out and sell door-to-door. The advantages for him were twofold; he had a cheap way of promoting our company and he had an inexpensive method to see if his "new" salesman was tough enough to survive the pounding necessary to get customers and be successful for the future. While this was hard on me, as far as advertising for the company was concerned it was a brilliant use of a cheap renewable resource. If I failed then nothing was lost.

It has been five years since we put up our company website and only recently did we come up with a real value-added proposition for our customers, primarily the largest telecommunications companies and their sub-contractors. We saw how much they were internally changing all of the time - growing, acquiring, spinning off. And we saw the problems all that activity created in label and parts design, revision management and product assembly. We thought that the best way that we could help was to create an interactive web site for each of them detailing all of their product codes, for labels, tags, cables, metal parts, etc. so that they could immediately access their most current drawings and art masters. With our customer's input we also added the ability to show proofs for new artwork and our current on-hand inventories. Another option was developed to show pictures of what finished products looked like so that people on the assembly lines could access the site, see what was supposed to go where and make sure that only the most recent issue of a drawing was utilized. We had no difficulty showing our customers that we could eliminate confusion and save them time and money.

We took the quality and inventory control issues out of the customers hands and put the responsibility squarely on us. It has become our responsibility to keep the sites current and make sure that our customers never run out of product. In this case, utilizing the "latest" communications forum, like the Internet has enabled us to help our customers in a direct, concrete manner that will save them time and money. In addition it avoids the inconvenience and embarrassment from having to do something over because of inadvertently using outdated components for their products.

But just having the hardware and software is not enough. With each customer site comes the need for continuous direct contact with the people involved. Telephone calls are great and are more personal than e-mail but there are times when you have to be face to face. Not just when you set up and close the deal but through the life of the project. People need to have a face or at least an image in their minds when they call. They need to know you personally and you have to be able to deal with them on a personal level.

Selling and marketing your company should be directly related to how you can offer help, convenience and efficiency to your customer base. The medium you choose to sell your product and service does not have to be focused on the most recent version of communication. It has to be chosen to best suit your needs and to get the best hit for your bucks. Don't be fooled by all the "dot.com" commercials. Most of those companies are already broke. Isolate yourself, your business and what you want and then decide what is best for you. Make your plan and then go do it. Personally I think carrier pigeons might be the next communication wave of the future, sometimes you just have to wing it.

NOTES

Chapter 37

It is OK to say nice job and you are doing fine.

Picked in the Middle for Basketball

12/24/2000

I talk to myself all of the time, some people may find that strange but I also supply the answers. Most of the time it is in a situation where I need motivation, either on the tennis court to go for a shot or in the office when I am not concentrating hard enough and I am either making mistakes or my mind is not working quickly enough.

When I was a little kid, somewhat overweight and not gigantically athletic I used to hate the games in school where the coach would pick the two best players and then the two captains would pick their teams. I detested those moments as I saw myself go further down the line with others picked over me. No one tried harder than I did but trying was enough.

As I got older my mouth sometimes grew faster than my ability to defend it which got me into some trouble. Eventually I came to the astounding conclusion, at least to me, that if I wanted to be picked further up the line in basketball, and be able to say what I wanted then I had better be in better shape and able to defend myself. It was time to put in the effort to justify and earn what I considered to be my rights.

I started to work out and as my body and mind improved I expanded the training across all areas of my life and I realized that the only person who was really going to look out for me was me. Sounds ridiculously simple don't it? I was the best one to promote my abilities and down play my weaker areas because I knew me best. I was also the one who would take the most interest in advancing myself forward.

What a concept, I was in it alone. If I wanted to achieve anything it had to come from within. If I wanted to learn how to sell it had to come from inside me. It did not matter what my boss/father said. It did not matter if he was pleased with how I did something; nothing mattered except that I followed my predetermined moral path of life and made my sales numbers at the end of the month. The rest was commentary.

We all have mentors, some positive and some negative. We have chosen them to act as our guides to life, but in any case by accepting their consul we have agreed to be judged. We want to please them and make them proud of us, to hear the words that declare that we have made it in any area that we have chosen. We can spend years or lifetimes striving to hear those words that will never come and we get frustrated, and saddened and angry because we can never hear the confirmation that we have made it.

Mentors are human, they have their good and bad traits and often one of their less desirable traits is that they are jealous of the people that they have mentored. It takes an extraordinary human being who can rejoice in the great deeds of a student that they have helped, let them know it and still remained untainted by their interior desires.

I know in my head that they just don't get it. But I suppose it is asking too much to get their information they are imparting and asking for acceptance also. This is why I become my own best cheerleader. It is why I tell myself I am doing a good job and I am proud of myself. It is why I do it first because it may not come from someone else, and after all who knows how well I did better than myself?

Having gone through the process myself I can see there are two ways to go. I can be a mentor, have incredibly valuable knowledge imparted to me, and let it stop there; or I can try to do better. I can add to it the final greatest gift that one human being can bestow on another and that is helping them to use the knowledge and then let them know they have done the job well and continuing to do it well as they improve. Mentoring is not a one shot job where you give it once and you are done, it is the continual helping, guiding and valuing of the person to let them know they are getting "it" and you are proud of them. Sometimes that only thing that someone needs is to hear that you have done a great job and not how the teacher would have done it differently or better.

I admit I have probably gone a little overboard with this. I am constantly telling the people who work for me, my family, customers and even strangers how great they are and how well they do something. I want people to get something positive from me even if it is nothing more than a smile and a good morning. We can all help, it doesn't have to be just with knowledge, but simply an uplifting of the soul which turns someone's day a little bit better.

I know in the end we are supposedly in this alone, but the training I have gone through has taught me that helping your brain, spirit and your body are all equally important. We all have to remember that we can help each in all areas and sometimes all it takes is to say good job and nothing else.

CHAPTER 38

Don't make it so easy to beat you.

Technologically Challenged

12/30/2000

My grandfather said he was too old to learn anything new. He retired in his early sixties, left by the wayside, because he refused to learn anything new. He had come to America when he was young man, learned a new language fluently and started his own business in 1921. He sold successfully through the Great Depression, World War II and Korea. By the time the 1950's rolled around he was successful, had two sons in the business and decided he had learned enough so he stopped growing. The world however did not and technology passed him by until there was no place left for him in business and he retired.

In the 1980's my Dad was not able to sell successfully any more, he was in his sixties but he kept learning. He taught himself about computers and helped to launch our company into the computer age far ahead of most others. When he could not sell he adapted and he learned something new which meant he could work productively until his early seventies when he chose to retire.

The world is changing faster all of the time, so why is it that I hear people saying they don't know how to use a computer or other new technology? New advancements are seen as the foreboding giant that is going to force the world into early retirement or cooking hamburgers because no one can keep up with the needed training.

Change is not something to be afraid of; it is a tool to be used. When my dad began to go into computers it was my view that we could start to utilize them as a replacement for people. Use them for the mundane tasks that most people did not want to do. Besides computers always showed up on time, even on Monday mornings and the days after vacations. They also did not get sick (except for an occasional "virus") or ask for raises or benefits. When computers get outdated they get replaced, which is unfortunately what happens to a great many people. As time went on and we broadened our use of them it became apparent just how much we were saving in time, efficiency and money.

At this point we have probably saved seventy-five percent of our labor costs because we have the newest technology. With the cost effectiveness of these new products it even becomes a question of whether to even bother having things fixed or just get new. Does this mean that there is no hope for people in the coming century?

In order to be able to survive and thrive does everyone have to be an expert in everything? The answer is of course not. But you are expected to be able to function within whatever system your company and your customer are is using. The excuse that you are computer illiterate or laugh off the fact that you do not have the latest technology is something I love to hear when competing against other firms, it means they are more easily beaten.

One of our greatest attributes is our ability to utilize new software and hardware that others have not or are not willing to put in. The ability to utilize the available information in new, more efficient and profitable ways for you and you customers is the major selling direction for this century. Most firms will be able to do similar tasks; it is those who can keep better control of costs, inventories, raw materials and data that will be able to capitalize on the faster, changing markets.

Customers are relying on their vendors to be able to control all aspects of business, and those who can handle it the most efficiently will be the one making the big bucks. Do I know all this technology myself? No, but I have people who do and I understand enough in the necessary areas to maximize its use for myself and the others around me.

Technology is only frightening if you allow yourself the luxury of being lazy and scared. You do not have either option in a marketplace that is prowling with people like me. I will compete with you on any level you like, but playing into my hand by being technologically backward is making it almost too easy.

If you made 10% more money now, would you be:

- ☐ ***Happier***
- ☐ ***Contented***
- ☐ ***Less Frustrated***
- ☐ ***Unchanged***

Why?

____

____

____

____

____

____

____

____

____

Chapter 39

You may know it in your head but not your stomach. In other words you may understand intellectually why something is so, but when put under fire your natural reactions point you in a different direction.

Why Is It So Hard?

6/29/2000

When I was just starting out in the family printing business my father told me that many things, especially in business were simple but not easy. I did not understand what he was talking about it until he threw me out on the road and told me to sell or die. Well, maybe he did not say sell or die but he made it clear that my worth to the family business was directly related to how well that I was able to take the stress and rejection of selling and be able to produce sales through my efforts.

What did he mean when he said simple not easy? He told me to go on the road, bang on doors, ask for the person who bought the printing, bring back any estimates for pricing, go back and try to close the deal. Then get the order, produce it correctly, on time and of good quality, get paid and then get more orders. It seemed simple enough, but what I just described took years for me to learn, internalize and then do it.

I think the secret is the internalizing. We often say a person understands it with their head but not their stomach. That means when the stress starts and you are put on the firing line, then what you know in your head evaporates and you are left with is the gut feelings in your stomach.

Often when you are starting out, those gut feelings reflect the primal urges from your youth. Depending on how you have related to past events, your initial reaction to a highly stressful situation could be to run, fight, become very quiet, talk too much, be embarrassed, become obnoxious etc., etc., etc. Worst of all is that these reactions will come out when you least expect and at the worst possible moments.

Here is an example.

You have been out trying to get new business for your new company. You have had appointment after appointment and while most people have been nice about saying no, others have not. You are getting increasingly worried that you will never get a customer until suddenly you find yourself in front of a buyer who could give you enough business to make you a success in your first year.

You know what you wanted to say, about your experience in his type of business in particular and in his field in general, how hard you wanted to work for him and make him look good. Everything you had practiced in your mind and in front of the mirror and you are ready to say it all. And you do say it all, unfortunately you were so nervous that you spoke non-stop for ten minutes, the entire time of the interview and never even breathed. The prospective client, who would have liked to ask a question or two at the beginning, while marveling at your ability to not breath, is by this time fed up. He smiles politely and shows you the door. The worst part was that you could see that you were irritating him and you could not stop yourself. Your mind was not in control , your stomach or primal needs were.

That is one of the keys to selling. Your stomach had taken over and you had stopped remembering, or were unable to remember why you were there. You job was to convince the customer that you could help him in any area he needed. But you were too busy thinking about yourself and what you needed. You had lost control and lost your chance for any business.

As I said, simple not easy. As you read this you can say to yourself that you would never let yourself get into that situation, you are control of your mind and emotions and can always count on yourself in times of stress. Bull!!!! Unless you have been on the firing line numerous times, you cannot ever hope to maintain control. This is not school and theory, this is the battlefield where your conduct will determine how far you will go.

Do you know why 90% of the people who sell make 10% of the money? Because they can't control their reactions and themselves. That 10% who make most of the money are people who know what has to be done and they do it on a consistent basis. They are able to take that raw emotional energy coming out of their guts and direct it to a positive area. They can funnel that energy to make it work for them in intelligent productive ways and they can drive the rest of the world into the ground because they have the key and know it.

There is no magic formula for being able to promote yourself and your company. You do not have to be the greatest designer, computer specialist or have a degree from the best college. What you have to know is what people need, fill that need and make your wants and desires secondary to theirs. You have to be able to recognize your faults, and try to at least neutralize, if not eliminate them and utilize your strength to the highest degree. The mere fact that you attempt to do this will put you on the road to greater wealth, prosperity and personal happiness. By the way don't forget to have fun while you are doing it. Being able to sell and promote yourself, when you can do it, is one of the most satisfying things you can ever accomplish. Every level you achieve is not only a step up on the financial ladder but a major move forward in your quest for inner happiness and spreading it to others.

You are going to make lots of mistakes, the people who don't are not trying. You will get more respect then you can ever imagine by starting and staying on this journey, it is the toughest and best challenge you will ever face and it will continue until you either give up or die happy.

Knowing yourself is the best way to see what you want to change and then doing it. You are not destined to make $40,000 or $400,000 a year. It is all up to you, once you have identified those internal emotions that are ready to rear up and kill you in stress situations, and bend them to your will to make them work for you.

You are at war, not with the world but with yourself, so don't take it out on everybody else, after all if it was simple and easy then everyone could do it.

NOTES

Chapter 40

You can do anything? Could you play first base for a professional baseball team? Is it your life's dream? The answer is of course you can. How? Buy the team. You don't have 500 million dollars? Go figure out a way to make it because even if you can't earn it by your physical talent alone your brain and dedication can get you the rest of the way. By the way, would you be satisfied with a minor league team—that could cost less than a million! You could be playing by next year.

You Are In Control

7/8/2000

I was in Temple this morning, I go to a weekly service that is run by the members, there are no clergy in charge. The people involved range from those that cannot read Hebrew and have only a small amount of education to those who are fluent and we even have two rabbis who are members.

Each week those of us in the select group who arrive first, decide who is going to run the service and give out the various other duties needed. This select group was not chosen by a committee, we were selected by the fact we felt comfortable enough to be able to run the service. Not only do you need to be able to read Hebrew well and know the service but you also had to be able to lead the group and that is the tricky part.

Whenever you get any amount of people, especially in a religious service, there is going to be a certain amount of "discussion" about how things should run. In fact many congregations have split apart with this issue as well as battles fought, countries created etc. So in essence, the leader is not only going through the material but is also running things and keeping order. In addition, he also decides on the speed and tempo of the service, when to read slow, fast, softly and loudly. The leader also decides what pitch to sing out which can make a lot of people very uncomfortable if they are singing outside of their normal voice ranges.

Put all this together and it is quite understandable why there are not a lot of people ready to lead. This morning was unusual as we had someone new. A nice woman, fluent in Hebrew, and seemed very capable. She was nervous and as we went through the service she made some mistakes and went too fast in some place and misses a few things but all in all she did a good job. Afterwards when heart rate returned to normal we all congratulated her successful trial by fire. She had become one of us and from this point on her new position was secured. I thought about what she had accomplished and I remembered Selling Rule #2: The most important thing to a person is their job and the 2nd most important thing is a better job.

She had taken a chance today to take herself out of the general congregation and step up to the group who lead. She did not have to do it, she wanted to, prepared for it and in the space of an hour changed her position in all of our eyes. Suddenly she was one of our group, now fully accepted to help choose leaders and participate as one in the future.

It is the same with everything else.

When I hired our current salesman he had been let go by a major corporation six months before. I told him that the moment he joined us, not only was he no longer unemployed but that he had risen far above where he had been before. He used to be a physical designer in a large company, a cog in a giant wheel, unnoticed and largely unappreciated. He was now a star, he was a salesman with a position and part of a seventy-nine year old business. He had power, and if he used it right, the ability to not only be very successful but to be a star in the view of the people who had let him go.

He was different from the moment I hired him, he made the jump in his body, mind and spirit and that transformed him from the unemployed to someone to be reckoned with. He went from someone without much confidence to a bull ready to do anything to prove to himself, to the world and especially to his former bosses that he had succeeded. He literally beamed as I worked him into the ground. I used every ounce of his physical and mental energy to forge him into the person he wanted to become. He was never happier or more tired in his life and he is doing well and he knows that it is a process that will never end as long as he keep wanting more in all areas of his life.

Like the woman in our Temple group he has been able to change his position because he accepted what it would take to do it, was willing to put forth the effort because he had a driving and consuming urge to succeed.

Who says you have to wait a certain amount of years for a promotion? Who says you cannot have you own business? Who says you can't change jobs and get a better situation. Only those people who judge themselves by your lack of success or by that little voice inside that says it is better to stay where you are than to risk making the leap for something a lot better.

You position in life in all areas is dictated by you. That covers everything including the mental, physical, spiritual, unconscious and primal parts. All these are mixed together to stop and start you from trying new things and going after new challenges. The idea that you would if you could but are stopped by anyone other than yourself is simply not true and just a crutch. We are all responsible for ourselves, our actions and whatever happens to us. Yes there "things" in life that happen both good and bad but on a percentage basis you are in charge of where you want to go, and if you can make it.

Remember the six rules of selling. They will help to focus your thoughts and structure your life to keep you centered on what is important.

Rule #1

Selling is the exchange of goods and services between one person and another.

Rule #2

You can never get what you want from someone else until you define first what they want and then satisfy their need. Only then will you have a chance of getting what you want in return.

Rule #3

The most important thing to anybody, apart from their family, is their job. The 2nd most important thing is a better job.

Rule # 4

You are there to do business never let your emotions get in the way of closing a deal.

Rule #5

If you are not prepared to put your life on the line then you will be beaten by someone who will.

Rule #6

Failure is not weakness.

Notes

Chapter 41

The ultimate in selling is having your customers think of you whenever they get into any type of trouble.

QUALITY-DEFAULT-ACTION

9/27/2000

The three most important things in real estate are location, location and location. The same can be said about promoting yourself, your ideas and your company. Where you locate yourself in the minds of your customers and prospects is critical to your success at influencing the selling relationship.

Many people think that the most important areas in business that buyers are concerned with are price, delivery, and service. I used to agree until, after years of battling for sales in American business, I came up with the *"Quality-Default Action"* strategy.

Whenever a stressful situation occurs, the number one priority of the person with the stress is to reduce it. I have found that if I can reduce the stress level for the other person *in any way* and keep doing it on a continuing basis, then that person will subconsciously start seeking me out whenever their stress level rises again. This does not involve price, service, product quality or design but is instead an all-encompassing emotional cage of stress that all buyers live in. By definition, to bring down their stress levels you have to supply a quality product or service in the time periods needed, but those are only the nuts and bolts of the situation. The overall path to selling is reduction of the buyer's stress level.

In promoting yourself, your ideas and your business, you can set up a physiological "default" mechanism in your customer's head to go off when they are involved with any type of tough situation so that hopefully, their first thought will be of you. In other words, if something bad happens and their assembly line stops or something good happens and production needs to be doubled immediately, they will come to you. Eventually, the second your customer's stress level jumps then you pop into their mind.

If you can successfully create this *Quality-Default-Action* relationship within your customer's mind then you will be the first one called which means that you will be the first to have a chance at fixing the situation thereby making your buyer and you look like stars. And that puts you in line for more business. If you respond quickly enough, you will be the first to get a shot at incredibly difficult, unusual, time sensitive items, and potentially profitable pieces of business and longer running jobs later on. You will also be the first one called when anything out of the ordinary happens which will keep you in the front of technological advancements in your industry. And it is at those moments when you are able to reduce the stress levels that it is the best time to lay the groundwork for - you guessed it - getting repetitive pieces of profitable business which means that you can afford that house, boat, family, or whatever you have always wanted.

To be able to put a customer into the *Quality-Default-Action* situation benefits them because it enables them to act rationally, quickly and intelligently in any given situation, by relying on you.

Here are some examples:

Situation 1: You have a potential new customer who calls and tells you that he has a new piece of business that is not in your area but is desperate and needs help to get it going.

Your answer can be:

1. *It is not in my area, I am not interested.*
2. *It is not in my area but I will try to help you, but not until I get the time.*
3. *It is not in my area but I will drop everything to help you because I know you are in trouble.*
4. *It is not in my area but I will drop everything to help you because I know that you are in trouble. And besides that, if you have a need for this product or service then maybe it is something I should be making so I can supply your need for now and the future.*

When I write it out like this it seems pretty obvious that if you were the buyer and your supplier answered with number 4, even if he did not produce, you would be happy with the enthusiasm, understanding of your needs and immediate responsiveness. As the supplier, at the very least, you would be far ahead of those competitors responding with either of the first 2 answers.

Too often in business people do not move fast enough. If you are in trouble then you want an instant response so at least you know that your crisis is being addressed. Just having someone say that they understand and will work on it right away is enough to begin reducing your level of stress. If your buyer knows you as someone reliable and truthful, that reduction in the stress level goes down a lot because you are working on his problem now. Understanding and using this view of things will make the help you provide a direct association between you and your customer and is the first step in attaining the *Quality-Default Action.*

Even if you cannot solve the problem, the more help you can give and follow-up support you can provide the more you will reinforce your trusted position.

Situation 2: You have a customer and you have screwed up his job. The customer calls you, desperate for help and information and you answer with the following:

1. *I will get to it when I have a chance; I am busy right now. Besides, it is not my fault.*
2. *I understand it is wrong but I can't get you an answer right away and I will have someone call you back.*

3. *I understand there is a problem and I will take care of it myself and will get back to you later.*
4. *I understand there is a problem and I am stopping everything to work on it. If it will help I will come over immediately (whether local or nationwide) and I will not stop until the problem is fixed. I am sorry for the trouble that I have caused you and your company and I will call you back every two hours, or as often as you would like, with updates until it is fixed.*

Again, the answer is obvious as to which reply, you as a buyer would like. Today's windows of opportunity for production and shipments are so tight that a buyer's job is often on the line when a mistake happens. When they call you with a problem their stress level is off the charts! If you can reduce that level they will associate you with the drop in stress, reinforcing the *Quality-Default-Action* relationship you are creating for them.

Often, during times of trouble you can not only fix the problem but by the way you handle it, keep the business and have a chance at more. The reason for that is that buyers know that if you do enough business, by definition some things will go wrong. Buyers will see how well you react under pressure and will want to be associated with someone who performs well in a crisis. It is great to say you guarantee your product. It is another thing to be there when havoc occurs because you made an error and an assembly line shuts-down. Trust is built over time and experience.

Situation 3: When the buyer has a problem from a mistake someone else made - my favorite situation!

The buyer is in trouble and asking for help and your answer is:

1. *I am busy right now but I can work on your problem in a few days.*
2. *I am busy but I will get someone else to work on it and they will call you tomorrow.*
3. *I can work on it immediately but I don't think there is anything that I can do.*
4. *I will stop everything to work on it right now and if I can't find a way to help you myself I will find someone who can. I will call you back with an update within 2 hours, if nothing else to tell you what I have been able to do so far.*

You are now getting the idea. It is obvious that if you were a buyer in trouble and your job was on the line you would pick option 4.

That approach not only helps to decrease the stress level of your buyer but keep in mind that anything you do is a positive and you have an opportunity to ride in like a white knight. Even if your buyer doesn't use your suggestions you will be associated with fixing things, a solution, a Quality-Default Action.

Please note that this has nothing to do with prices. The customer is in trouble and needs help now; money is not an issue! Getting the items fixed, changed or a new product introduced is the key. However, be cautious here. Although money is not the customer's main concern, make sure they have an idea of what it will cost before going ahead. It is much harder to justify a price after the crisis has passed and the people in accounting are questioning your bills.

Your desire is to promote yourself, your ideas and your company. Your job is to have other people buy whatever it is that you are promoting. Your goal is to have a constant stream of people who will buy what you have. The vehicle to do all of that is a Quality-Default-Action strategy for your customers and prospects that gives them a stress reducing solution to their problems that they can turn to on a continuing basis.

If you made 10% less money than you do now, but liked your job more, would you be:

- ☐ ***Happier***
- ☐ ***Contented***
- ☐ ***Less Frustrated***
- ☐ ***Unchanged***

I am jealous of people who make more money than I do because:

____

____

____

____

____

____

____

____

____

____

____

Chapter 42

It is not a mentor if they don't talk back

You Have To Answer To Someone Who Can Answer Back

6/16/2002

Selling is a wonderful way of life, besides giving you a vehicle to be able to make all your dreams a reality it gives you something else that is almost as important: It listens and answers back.

When you are trying to market and sell yourself you are dealing with people on all sides of the business equation all the time. In fact, if you are dedicated to becoming or staying successful then most of your waking moments are centered on trying to figure out how to do everything better, be more efficient, and make more money. The great part about the world is that they will answer you back. I don't mean that someone will tell you when you have been outsold, underbid or out maneuvered by your competition. They give you a concrete negative indicator, when you don't get the business, and a positive one when you do. You know when you have done it right or not.

I have a friend, and he is a Rabbi. I have watched him as my friend and Rabbi, over the last eight years rise, from a new assistant to the head of one of the biggest congregations in the country. He is amazing in front of people, his ability to put people at ease, help them to learn, comfort and confront them when necessary. Yes, he can even get stubborn people like me to think and re-evaluate my positions, he is very good. He has got almost everything that he wants including a beautiful, understanding wife, great friends and a congregation that adores him. Unfortunately he is missing the one important ingredient, that without it could cost him everything.

That "thing" he is missing is that he has no one to answer to. The person he declares that is his only true boss does not answer him back directly. While God oversees his work and his life, in the earthly sense he stands alone to lead his congregation both as a spiritual and business leader of a multi-million dollar operation. He is surrounded and enveloped in the details of not only the spiritual betterment of his flock but the business of running the Temple to keep it a thriving growing profitable enterprise.

When my wife and I were last out with them, in the space of a couple of hours he got at least 6 phone calls, and this was a Saturday night. I was sitting next to him and it sounded like he was being electrocuted because his cell phone vibrator kept going off. He is on constant call and is not willing or able to see what the job, both the business and spiritual is doing to him.

Being in charge is a fun, invigorating and a challenge. I love the thrill of being able to make things happen, I often feel that the energy that soars through my body is a gift from God. I know that people often take drugs to try and feel that way that I do from a natural high that I get from life. But that high comes at a price which is that I have to keep my mind, body and soul in top shape at all times. All parts of my being have to be heading in the same positive direction in order to create that energy explosion.

But as much as this comes from inside me I also know that as a boss and leader I still have to have people to answer to. You have to have people who can see from the outside the results of your actions whose opinions you trust enough to be able to alter what you do from their reactions. I answer to two people who have the ability to monitor and modify my life. No one likes criticism but you need people to ground you so that you stay on the best paths. Listening to them is the important thing, like my wife at home and my head of operations at work, both have the ability to make me stop, stand back and make a reality check to make sure I am going in the right direction for all concerned.

I had a dream about my friend last night. He was being taken away in an ambulance the victim of something like a stroke or heart attack and later I was bringing him some place. He then disappeared and I did not see him again. It scared the heck out of me because I realized that he would not place his trust in the people around him to set-up checks and balances, he is working alone.

He is also working himself to death, not taking care of himself healthwise and will listen to no one, only God and unfortunately the only time that God will answer him back directly will be when it is too late. No one can stand-alone and be able to maximize all of their potential. We all need feedback both good and bad and the ability to take the information, internalize it rationally and act on it. And if that means to eat right, exercise and find ways of getting help to relieve the stress load than we had better do it.

My friend is one of the "best" people I have ever met, I cannot not stop him, I can't help him because I cannot even get him to listen. I do not want him to disappear like in my dream, and out of all of our lives. But he is travelling a path I cannot stop because he is travelling it alone.

Chapter 43

Life is full of opportunities that come and go in a split second-if you are not ready you can never recognize or capitalize on them.

You Get One Chance

4/22/2001

Another person died last week, the winter had been too rough and his age, he was ninety-seven finally caught up with him. I barely knew him except to nod a hello when we met in Temple. But he was the dad of our friends and of course my wife and I went to the funeral.

Some funerals you know are going to be really tough, where the person who passed was young or had died tragically, but in this case, although there had been some very tough times, his life overall seemed to have been rich and fulfilled. Therefore, I was not expecting a lot of people crying and showing large amounts of emotion.

My friend, the Rabbi of our congregation delivered the eulogy, he is an artist with the spoken word and he illustrated one of the fundamentals of selling without realizing it.

One week ago when my friend went to see the dying man in the hospital and they both knew that his end was coming soon. The Rabbi looked at the man and asked him two questions. The first was, "Are you in pain?" For which he nodded no. The second was "Do you know how well you did during your life?" In other words did the man understand that as a direct result of his living the life the way he chose, did he realize how many people he had impacted positively?

The man understood the question and smiled and nodded, he knew what he had done, was happy with the life he had led and was also grateful for the Rabbi for having pointed it out, especially right before he was about to pass on.

Never ask a question if you are not prepared for the answer. A common bit of advice but one which so few people heed. How many times have you been asked something by someone and they have been surprised when you not only tell them your answer but also get upset at the question? If the dying man had said that he was not contented and was not at peace then there was no time to do anything about it. My friend would have been left with the knowledge that not only did the man know that he did not die at peace, but he would also know that Rabbi knew it also. It was a chance, or was it? I don't believe my friend even consciously considered the possibility of a negative answer, he had read the situation, the people involved, and went with his gut instinct.

When someone asks me "how are you? Most people really don't want to know the true answer; they are just filling in space until they can get to talk about what they really want, which is what interests them. The real geniuses in selling in any area are the people who can see, feel and hear, not only what people are saying, but the vibrations they are giving off in the context of that moment and translate those signals into spoken words that can utilize that data and move their customers and potential customers to positive action.

Although the day to day activities of everyone (and everyone is selling all of the time) is not nearly so important as someone's last days on earth, they still are of great importance to the people involved. If their son just lost an important little league game, or their company just cut 5% of its work force, or they are about to be considered for a promotion, is all very important to the person with whom you are dealing.

Your opinions, wants and desires really mean very little when it comes to selling. Your ego strength is irrelevant to the person you are trying to sell, except in supporting his. Your job is to define the need, what the person wants and help fulfill that desire in whatever way is possible as long as it does not impact your moral code, sense of justice or fair play. Your job is to create an arena where sales can take place and you can't do that from the "I" position, it can only be done from your customer's point of view.

Remember that in this world of non-absolutes you are working with a few universal truths that you can bank on. The first is that the biggest concern to your buyer is his job and his way of life. The next most important thing is a better job and the third thing you can be sure of is that all events they experience will be filtered through their "I" filter. This means that they will judge events as they effect them first.

The only other universal truth is that life is based on percentages and if you keep trying to do something in a rational, constructive way that is based on utilizing your strengths and solving the problems of your customers, in any area, then you are quarantined a rate of success based on your abilities and willingness to keep going.

Keep your eyes and feelings open to the signals being given off by your environment and you will maximize that percentage rate and decrease the amount of time it takes to reach your goals.

Chapter 44

You want to sell? What happens if it works?

What To Do With Customers Once You Get Them

8/3/2000

You have been working on breaking open one particular account for a year and half and you finally get your first order. You produce it, it is delivered in whatever shape or form "it" is, then you sit back and wait for the deluge of new business to come in.

Assuming that you produced whatever it was you were supposed to in an acceptable period of time, on budget and within an acceptable quality level, then why should you not figure that you would then be in line to get every piece of business your new customer has to give? That would seem reasonable, right?

Wrong!!!! Getting a second order is almost as tough as getting the first, which is a little tougher then getting the third order. You can never stop selling. You can never rely on the good works of the past. You have constantly got to be in the mind of your customer in order even to be considered for the next piece of business.

Let's dive into the mind of a typical buyer for a moment. How can we accurately predict what they are thinking? That is easy because they are human. According to the 2nd rule of selling, "the most important thing to a person is his job and the 2nd most important things is a better job."

Therefore, since buyers are people, we can be sure that they are most concerned with their job. That means their job is dependent on doing what is expected of them which usually includes getting high quality goods and services at the best possible price in the shortest lead times. They are also responsible to insure that their assembly and production lines do not stop and that they have people that they can count on when they get into trouble.

Most good buyers will constantly be trying other new vendors in anticipation of the company introducing new product lines or to insure that in case of trouble they will be covered. They have their favorite suppliers that they are loyal to and send the bulk of their business. The buyer's loyalty is a good thing because you want them to be loyal to you when it is your turn. Your job is to win that trust and then do everything in your power to keep it.

The odds are good that if you got a first order one of the following has happened with your customer:

❶ *The buyer is new and is trying to create his own new vendor base.*

2. *The buyer is experienced but has problems with his current suppliers in the price, delivery or service area and is checking out potential vendors to keep in reserve or replace a failing vendor.*
3. *The buyer is teaching one of his main vendors a lesson by pulling some business from him and giving it to a "new" guy to show him he is not too dependent on the original supplier.*
4. *The buyer has an emergency and his current suppliers do not have the ability to get him through it.*
5. *The buyer has a new piece of business or some new need for which there is no current supplier and he has to source it.*

What chances do you have with options like these? The answer is "plenty."

The first order is indeed the toughest but it is easier to get a second order than to go out and get a new customer.

When I was just starting out in selling my father told me to go "cold calling" which meant I was banging on doors of companies and asking them for business. It was a painful, difficult process filled with a lot of rejection. But I learned a lot about myself and one of the main things was that I loved to sell and that I was good at it. I was soon breaking open large new accounts, wowing my Dad and my compatriots and feeling on top of the world. Unfortunately, I was losing these accounts as fast as I got them because I did not know how to service my customers. I was not thinking about them, I was thinking about what I wanted, which was the thrill of the first victory, and therefore most of my first orders became last orders.

Over time I realized that the only way to get multiple orders, pieces of business and larger, more profitable accounts was to understand the needs of my customers and fulfill them as quickly and consistently as I could.

I tried to keep in touch with them and send them samples as often as possible - but not too often.

My goal was to become the "can-do" vendor for my clients. Whenever anything went wrong or something new came up I wanted them to think of me as a solution. It is not something that happens in a day or a week or even a year but over time it can be done. One order means nothing except a boost in ego and the signal to keep going. The only true measure of success is a long term working relationship that benefits your customer in his quest to keep his job and get a better one and yours to build your sales, your company, your bank account, and your future.

So what do you do now? You got the first order and that is fantastic, but your job really just began. Now is your chance to become the specialist in the mind of your customer, the person they can call whenever they are in need or in trouble. It is at this point, after the first order, where they will probably take your call, answer your e-mail and treat you like a human being, unlike the way many of them treated you before. Capitalize on your ticket to ride. That first order is your chance for the golden ring but remember you are walking a very fine line. It only takes one instance to anger your customer with too many phone calls or attention. You are walking a tightrope between being kept in mind and being a pain in the neck. The only way to find out is to "walk the walk" and make the mistakes. If, over time you are not getting enough clients, you are probably being too timid or are not working hard or smart enough. If you are being told to go away, maybe you are pushing too hard or are not working hard or smart enough. Everyone is different and you have to find your own level, the odds are good no one will actually tell you what you are doing wrong so you will have to judge it by your percentage of success.

The first sale is the toughest but the repeat business is what counts. Blowing it by being too aggressive or not aggressive enough can make you sick but you have no choice because unless you are making one-call closings with door-to-door encyclopedias, you cannot make a living out of only getting first orders.

Remember you are doing the hardest thing imaginable in the world, selling. You should take great delight in just being able to think about doing this let alone acting on it. Whatever happens, don't be too hard on yourself or anyone else, you need time and patience, and combined with a good sense of humor you will hopefully get closer to your dreams.

NOTES

Chapter 45

Some call it obsession, others call it crazy, I call it commitment, and the best way to happiness.

Commitment To Yourself

6/16/2002

You cannot reach your dreams unless you can launch a long term sustained focused attack consisting of all parts of your being, mind, body and soul. Your body has to be in good enough shape to give you the energy to fuel your journey and be able to supply whatever power bursts are needed.

If you are not in great shape mentally, physically and spiritually then you will be beaten, on a percentage basis by someone who will.

Buy yourself a calendar. It is not for your vacations days, it is a place to structure your life, to commit that you will exercise on whatever days you decide, keep to whatever type of diet you decide, and will attain whatever areas of advancement you aspire to on a particular date or month.

Life consists of levels, you have to mass your reserves to be able to make the effort to reach the next plateau. No one can do it for you. You need to be able to think with a clear head and have your goals pre-thought out so that when the opportunities present themselves, and they will, you will take advantage of them. You have to be ready, you have to practice and you have to do it on a consistent long-term basis. You are in a battle to maximize whatever is inside of you and it begins now. You are fighting against people like me, who have been trained form birth to go after what we want and are willing to do almost anything, on a high moral plain, to get it.

You can do this, you just have to make the commitment and start now.

Declare in one month that you will do the following:

> ***Body:*** *Exercise-decide how many times a week, where, and for how long (check your doctor first)*
>
> *What kind of fuel are you putting into your body? Good food=good fuel=lots of energy.*
>
> ***Mind:*** *If you are not already doing it. Pick two books to read now, one a biography of someone you admire, the other a biography of someone's success you would like to emulate. Resolve to have them read within 45 days and keep track!*
>
> *Put a pad and paper by your bed-start writing down your ideas about everything. The next day transfer them all to a master list.*
>
> *Review your list every day, if the ideas still seem good after a week, put them into action. If you did not have a good brain you would not have gotten this far, have faith in your ability to succeed and keep going!*

Read newspapers, listen to public radio, try and figure out why people do what they do. Do people do things in their own best interest? Do you?

Soul: *Do something nice for someone else. Try to go to the temple or church of your choice at least once a month. Take up yoga or some type of spiritual outlet.*

Do something to help the inner you that most of us ignore. Let yourself think about everything and nothing. Listen to yourself breathe and relax, try not to take it all so seriously and remember to laugh.

Don't think that my life is an easy, straight highway. No matter how successful anyone gets, there is always lots of "stuff" going on. Having a calendar will help you to create a structure and plot your progress. Write down the goods and the bads, keep a journal to channel your journey, your new life is beginning.

Do you think you are paid fairly for the work you do?

Would you work harder if you got more money?

CHAPTER 46

What assets do you have? Take stock in yourself regarding your mental, physical, emotional and financial well being and then read about Daman.

Daman the Cab Driver

8/6/2000

Recently, while on a vacation trip to Bermuda, I had planned to take a bus from one end of the island to another. I was on my way to a lesson on how to blow glass; I am always looking for a new hobby. I was going to take a bus because the cabs were so expensive, but as usual I got bored and tired quickly of waiting. I decided to forget about the money and take a taxi.

As I got into the cab the driver was busy on his cell phone. Most of the taxi drivers on the island made a determined attempt to get along with their passenger and while at first I felt a little ignored I soon began to enjoy the silence and the passing gorgeous scenery of the sand and the surf.

As he got off the cell phone, the cab driver, named Daman focused his attention on me and we began to talk. It seemed that he loved his work. You don't normally think of taxi drivers as loving their work but Daman did. When I asked him why he said it was because he owned the cab and was his own boss.

He had worked as a hospital worker and although the pay and benefits had been good, he was not satisfied. So he worked for two years, nights, holidays and weekends for someone else in order to save up to buy his own cab and go in to business.

With his newly purchased car he could have worked for someone else or for a big taxi service, but Daman had to be alone. He wanted the freedom to work the twelve hours a day or whatever it took to attain the living standard he desired. He worked because he wanted to, not because he was ordered. The cell phone suddenly rang again; he was conducting business, as his taxi was his office. Then, once again, he was centered on me. Like most entrepreneurs he almost glowed as he spoke about his company, how hard he worked and how proud he was of his success.

I got the feeling that he would have done absolutely anything in order to be successful. It was not just the difference in money, he earned three times more owning his own cab than working for someone else but the fact that he was in charge of his life, his destiny and he had no plans of ever going back the other way.

I am the son of a son of a printer. My father worked for my Grandfather, then was in partnership with his brother and finally by himself. I went to work for my dad in 1977, he said I was the only one in the world he would ever take the time and pain to train. Eventually we became partners and were together until he retired three years ago. He could never have gone back to work for anyone again, and although I consider myself incredibly disciplined, I also know how hard it would be for me.

Being an entrepreneur has it pluses and minuses. The negative is that if you are never able or willing to take the plunge and go in for yourself, then you will spend your life wishing that you had tried. You will probably second-guess every boss you will have because you know, in your heart that you could do better or at least differently. It is like a fever or festering sore within you that will never go away, because you yearn for the chance to call the shots and go your own way. The trouble is that as time goes on and your responsibilities mount it becomes harder to make the attempt.

While the rewards can be great the downside is extreme. You will have to pledge your heart, soul, brain, house, bank account and your future. For those around you they too have to make the commitment to back you as the odds are good you will not make it. Your commitment must be total or you will be beaten by someone who is.

Most new companies fail. Their owners either did not have perseverance, knowledge, experience, financial backing or guts to see their dream through. It is an exciting, scary, petrifying wonderful journey and not for those who scare easily.

But if you are truly an entrepreneur then the rest doesn't matter. You will find someway to make it work, to safeguard what you hold dear and reach the level that you are capable of. Unfortunately, this doesn't mean it will happen on the first, second or even third try. The only guarantee you have is that if you keep trying you will get to the point where you failed the last time and it will force you to break through before so you can reach your next level.

The 2nd rule of selling states that the most important thing to a person is his job the 2nd most important thing is a better job. In the case of an entrepreneur his eyes and his heart are on only one thing and that is having his own business. The biggest mistake that you can make is trying to hold them at a place where they are not destined to be.

Chapter 47

Just like football, golf or computer programming every type of business and occupation has a "type" of person who does best in it. There is always a certain combination of traits that "genetically" selects a person to have the best chances of success in that area. Don't worry if you want to sell and these do not describe you, many things can be learned and besides this is my opinion and I have been wrong before.

The Ten Traits of a Salesman

1/13/2001

I was just visiting the Smithsonian Air and Space Museum with my eldest son Ben when I realized something. As I looked at most of the flying machines that people had developed and flown through the years I was struck by , not only the magnitude of their achievements, but the size of their vehicles. How could people go hundreds and thousand of feet off of the ground surrounded by materials you could punch through with a screwdriver. The plane that flew around the world without refueling looked like it had the inside room of a sawed off minivan and those people were in there for days.

To me that would seem like a prison sentence that would be close to unbearable. Being cooped up in a small place for a long period of time sounds awful to me.

My brother is a dentist and spends his day happily inside people mouths helping them to have less pain and improving their lives. He does a wonderful job, as I can personally attest to, but again doing that myself with the sound and smell of the drill going through teeth all day would make my skin crawl.

What do I do for a living? One of my primary jobs is to sell and that, to most people is the worst possible job to have. The thought of having to talk and go after people who want nothing to do with you on a continuing basis for years is so abhorrent that during the Great Depression people would rather go on assistance then answer the newspaper ads for salesman.

Why is selling considered a horrible profession? Possibly because of the bad reputation of used car and insurance salesman who in many cases seem less concerned with their customers than making their sales quotas. The idea of being associated with "those " types of people who are pushy and aggressive is too much for the egos of most.

Another problem is that sales is one of the few professions where there is the chance that the boss will want you to go on commission. That means if you don't sell enough, you won't make money. There are no guarantees, which means that you have nothing solid upon which to build your future.

Then there is the third fear, that if you are too successful, then your boss will fire you and take your accounts. Overnight, years spent building up your customers will be lost, and then it will be back to square one.

The problem is that all of these fears are justified, they can happen and all of the horrible things that they say about salesman can also be true. So why should anyone voluntarily go into this field when so many bad things that can go wrong? The answer is the money. Selling is the fastest way to go from being poor to successful. It is the quickest way to realize your dreams and change your circumstances in a way that you choose. It is also the best way to impact other people lives in a positive and enduring way. In short, it can be the way to fulfill your dreams and the people around you.

How do you know if you have the "basics" for sales? Here is my top ten list for the best traits to have to be successful in selling.

Paranoid: to be able to watch out for the people who will do you harm so you can avoid and take advantage of them as the situations arise.

Optimistic: which may seem in direct opposition to number one, but it isn't because you need to be able to view life as an upbeat place where you can be positive and help others to improve their lives.

Detail Oriented: you need to be able to take care of the small stuff so you can concentrate on the large. Those little details like deciding what to wear, your route to work, what days and where to work out, what to have for breakfast; should all be pre-thought out and preplanned so that you can go on automatic pilot. You have to complete the basics on a daily basis so you can concentrate on the large stuff like making sales to get you successful.

See what other people see: you need to also center on the small stuff of other people. Those little things will define where they will spend their time. If you can see where they focus, then you will have a better understanding as to what makes them tick. The more you understand about them the better your chances of selling your products and services.

Know your product lines: make yourself a specialist as soon as possible, know as much as you can so you can help your customers and your boss to shine.

Have fun: No one wants to be around anyone who hates their job. If you do not like people, do not like changing peoples lives for the better, do not like the challenges of an incredibly changing marketplace where you can affect everything, get out of the business because you are wasting your time.

Have a plan: What do you want? When do you want it? Who do you want to help besides yourself? How are you going to do it?

Passion: You have to have it, like a driving force that will bring you the ability to maximize whatever natural and acquired talents that you have.

Have a thick skin: Don't let what other people say about you, matter except to help motivate you to do a better job than you have ever done before. Again, this will maximize your chances to get what you want.

Less Fear: Don't be afraid to make a fool of yourself, allow yourself the freedom to do things that probably will not work but do them anyway even if you look dumb. I cannot tell you how many times I have tried stuff that did not work, but it doesn't matter because in the end people remember the success so that, on a percentage basis, if you keep going with intelligent attempts you will succeed to whatever you talents merit.

Few can sell, even fewer can be at the top but don't let what others think and feel cloud your view. If you think you have a chance it is your fastest and cleanest way to get whatever you want at the speed that you are able to handle it.

NOTES

Chapter 48

Don't feel sorry for them, be envious at their incredible courage.

The Immigrants

8/17/2000

My wonderful wife decided that it was time for us to have a new kitchen. So a few days ago I came home to a house in controlled havoc. What was before a kitchen was now a blank room, the doors had plastic sheeting over them to cut down the dust and our dining room was going to serve as a makeshift kitchen/dining room/meeting area for the next six weeks.

In order to get a new floor a new base of cement had to be put down first and when I came home last night there was an older man, about 60 years old waiting in our driveway to be picked up. His face was lined and showed the signs of a life of hard wear. My wife was waiting for me; my daughter had not wanted to leave because she did not want the old man to be left alone. His ride had been delayed and he looked sad and she felt sorry for him.

We checked on his ride and realized that he would be waiting a while so I got him an apple and a chair and he calmly waited happily. It was a beautiful evening, he spoke no English and we communicated by sign language. My daughter had felt sorry for him because he seemed alone in a strange world without even the ability to communicate.

I went out for a walk and as I came back down the hill I passed a little old lady. I was trying to be quiet so I would not scare her and as I went by her, she was barely moving, she smiled with a determined look and in a Russian accent said she was jogging.

My grandfather came to this country when he was eleven years old. Within a very short time he learned English well enough that he lost his accent. He held three jobs and eventually started his own business, which would eventually become mine.

I remember feeling as my daughter did when I was a young boy. People who had come to this country, seemed out of place, lonely and having a tough time, far from their homelands and their family's starting new lives and carving out new destinies derived from their own initiates.

It is the immigrants that helped to forge this country into what it is. It is that steely nature of that little old lady saying she was jogging although she was barely moving. It was that man laying out kitchen floor with a skill he probably learned fifty years ago in another country across the world. It is that attitude of not caring what it takes, they are going to succeed and get a better life for themselves and their children.

I should not have felt sorry for them when I was a boy and my daughter should not now. They got what they wanted, the chance to succeed even if it meant risking their lives to get it.

That chance to "make it" is all so often forgotten by those of us who were born here. Many of the kids today have never seen bad times or even rough ones so how could they possibly appreciate what they have?

Our views that the young know more than the old, they can learn faster and better and there is no place for anyone over 40 is ridiculous.

Just because you cross the forty-year line doesn't mean that your life has ended. Many of today's workers and middle managers who will lose their jobs in the next economic downturn or merger will feel lost and unwanted. They will feel that their skills are worth less than the young and that they have been priced out of the market. They don't think they can compete especially with their added responsibilities of family's to support. They feel that they don't have a chance.

No chance? They are citizens; they have the ability to learn and try new things, the freedom to do as they will, something the immigrants have literally risked their lives for. In our office many of the people are over forty, in fact I look for older people because they have a seasoned, rational view of life and the ability to handle the ups and downs as they occur. Yes they can cost more, but they will also often be more loyal and willing to try different things.

The main thing is to make sure that the older you get the more you strive to learn and keep up. The learning curve will continue to increase and those who stay with it and surpass it, not matter what age you are, will be ensured of better positions then those who sit back and rest at whatever point they are.

You are never too old; when my Dad was sixty years old he taught himself about computers and became a major asset to our company because of his ability to integrate and manipulate computer systems to maximize our efficiency.

People who are knowledgeable, intelligent, industrious and have a passion to do a good job will always find a place no matter what the economy is like, it is up to you to keep yourself in that position. The immigrants, like my grandfather, never lost their focus where it mattered and it is a lesson we all need to relearn everyday.

CHAPTER 49

Sir Isaac Newton was right, for every action there is an equal and opposite reaction. The same goes for life, things generally equal out. The more good that you do, the more good that will come to you with the opposite also being true.

The Best and the Worst

1/7/2001

I was minding my own business the other day and it suddenly occurred to me that everything was going great and I was happy, contented and moving on schedule. The next thought was of sure panic because I knew that as good as things were at that moment, then surely something was going to mess it up.

My next reaction was anger that I was trying to sabotage my happiness and I forced myself to believe that things did not have to go wrong. But I was lying to myself and I knew it because my life runs in streaks.

Our company is ISO 9002 and 14001 registered which means that we operate under a set of international quality and environmental standards that insures that we operate at prescribed levels. Those registrations were brutally hard to get and we were one of the first printers in the United States to have both. Both systems are audited by outside inspectors twice a year, which means that we have auditors in our place four times a year. They have the option to look anywhere and do anything to anyone that they want. It is understandable that we are a little crazy just before each time we are checked.

Those certifications mean a great deal to our marketing ability and we are very careful to insure we do nothing that would risk their continuance. We had an audit coming up, therefore we spent the last week getting ready. I was a little more concerned than usual when it began, as our preparations had not gone as smoothly as I had hoped. Up until this point my streak of good fortune had been intact which was another reason I was poised for a disaster.

As the audit went on it became apparent that we were happily ready for it and we concluded it successfully in a very short time. An hour after the elation of the successful conclusion was finished "it" hit the fan. A few years ago we had created an ink match for one of our customer's colors and I thought that the customer had given us the formula. As it turned out he had not and I had mistakenly attributed that ink color to him for years. While it did not cause a great deal of problem for my customer, so little in fact that we did not even have to do anything other just agree to fix it for the future, that to many it would have seemed like a little wrinkle.

To me however, it was a disaster. Something I had been so sure of for years was suddenly wrong and it was my responsibility for not having checked it more thoroughly when we started. I sunk into a grand funk, as far down as I had been up before.

Although this mistake did not cause a great deal of trouble, it severely bothered me because not only did I feel badly for it and the small amount of problems it caused, but also because I knew it was the answer for having everything else go so right. When all is said and done, everything always comes down to three things which are fate, the odds and the good you put in.

If I am a better person at work, home and to all people than I am creating good will that will come back to me later. If I am involved in a situation that has developed differently than I planned than I have to look at it that fate has given me a different set of options and I have to work from there. For instance I had planned to work out in my office last Saturday, but I had forgotten my warm-up bag. I almost never do that so I figured I was being told to do something else. So then I tried to go cross-country skiing later and right before I got started my ski binding broke. At that point I got the idea to go bicycling and I did. Was someone telling me not to go cross country skiing and if so why did it happen before I got started as opposed to miles from my car when I could have been in trouble in the woods.

Also, was I meant to go bicycling which just happened to go past my office which enable me to stop in while riding and talk to my 2nd in command who was in on that Saturday afternoon? I don't know, but I do know that the more I follow with the options that are presented to me, instead of fighting or ignoring them, then the better and more smoothly things seem to happen.

I like to work at the odds. I believe and hope they stop me from getting into big trouble. Atlantic City and Las Vegas are in business and making lots of money, not because they are lucky for the owners, but because of the odds. They never stop working over time. You may have a momentary change but in the end they will always equal out. This means that in life things will even out, the good and the bad. The best that you can do to increase your odds of good things is by only putting positive things into it. If you want to have as good and happy a life as possible then act in a good and happy way. Be nice to people and it will come back to you, treat them fairly and with respect and they will do it back to you, mostly. There will always be some bad, but if you work hard enough you can move the centerline toward the good side.

Happily, the bad thing that happened to me was not a disaster and, through fate, is probably going to stop me from doing or having something even worse happen to me later. Perhaps that formula was a reminder for me not to get cocky or to be more careful and make fewer mistakes or something else that I don't even know about. It is comforting to think that maybe someone is looking out for me, guiding me towards a better life. I know that good luck comes to people who work for it through their thoughts and action. I also know that I can never move that time line to insure that nothing bad will happen, but at least I can nudge it a little bit more toward the positive so those bumps in the road hopefully don't become mountains.

Chapter 50

It is often hard or impossible to see where "you are." Sometimes a "friend" has to point it out.

Ready to Leap

7/19/2001

I made one of my best friends cry this morning and I feel like a big jerk. Every Sunday morning I walk with "Uncle Dave". He is not really a relative (actually our family adopted him by making him my eldest son's godfather) and he is truly part of us. He is also, like me, involved in printing and since we are both "bosses" son's and grew up in our family's businesses we share that additional connection. The big difference between us is that he struck off on his own, left his father early in his career and began his own company while I stayed with mine.

Uncle Dave is a fantastic person. He's probably the best personal networker I have ever met and the only man I know who can make endless cold calls on companies which means knocking on potential customers doors without appointments and asking to speak to the buyer. It is a grueling, low percentage way of getting sales but he is able to go back, time after time with a 3% entry success rate and make it work. I marvel at his ability to persevere, no matter what people throw at him and go back for more.

But he does have an area where he has not excelled and that is in his belief system and his own abilities and self worth. For anyone to be able to market and sell themselves to their maximum potential they have to be able to accurately gauge their assets and liabilities and sell their better parts in the strongest way possible. If you downplay your abilities then the potential customers have no choice but to believe your own advertising and judge you the way you rank yourself. It is like when I was dating - if I saw a woman I thought was really beautiful, and she did not think of herself as good looking, then she would eventually convince me that she was right. You can call it confidence, arrogance or a belief system but whatever self-image you have is what you broadcast to everyone else.

I believe in Dave's abilities more than he does and I think that he can do absolutely anything including the hardest part of selling which is to open up the initial contacts. The trick is for him to believe he has more to offer than someone who sells a product for a cheap price and adds nothing else. People don't just buy things or services - they buy trust. A sale is a contract between two people and boils down to one person trusting another to deliver a product or service at the terms agreed upon and when they say it will be done. Everything else is just "commentary" if the product is late or doesn't function correctly.

A customer's assembly line can go down and someone's job can be at risk and it is at those moments that buying the cheapest product at any cost is not paramount in a buyer's mind. If a salesman is just selling product then he is not putting himself on the line regarding the responsibility to service the customer in whatever ways are necessary to help safeguard the buyers job and a chance at a better one.

If the seller does not want to get personally involved and resists providing what is really needed, which is putting himself on the line, then he deserves the lower profit levels that come with no risk taking or extra effort. The buyer is paying for support whether he's purchasing new technology or placing re-orders. When times get tough he and his staff need to be able to rely on someone to help him stay out of trouble by providing help when and where it is needed.

Although Dave provides the support customers crave through his willingness to do anything to make sure they are taken care of, he doesn't believe his abilities should be the basis for his selling and making more money. When he goes to talk to buyers he speaks with them from a position of weakness because he emphasizes the safe, easy things, like cheap prices and the same things that everyone else sells. He does not talk about the higher level service he provides, or his expertise in other areas, like helping his customers to get more sales and maximize their potentials, all of which the customer really wants to know about. Some salespeople can sell at a high level, and treat buyers as people who have specific needs that must be met in order to sell them on a higher plane, but most can't and they are left to wander in a world of lower profit, less important and lower pressure product lines. The most important thing to a buyer is his job and the next most important thing is a better job. If a salesman cannot define what actions need to be taken to help with those primary interests of the buyer then he will either be relegated to cheap and inconsequential products or replaced by someone who can think and act on a higher level.

Telling someone they are not living up to their potential is very hard. If they are ready to move to the next level and start selling on a higher plane then you are touching a raw nerve which will generate very strong emotions and reactions such as getting angry. In sales as in life we all try very hard to get "better" but the experience is usually so frustrating that it undermines our self-esteem and confidence. But a single, final emotional response to the frustration, like crying, actually means that you are ready to make the next jump to a higher level.

You don't have to be a genius to know when you have reached a new level of performance. You will realize it from the reactions of the people around you, in addition to making more money and being happier than you have ever been before. I made my friend cry and for him I am glad because I can see what is about to happen even if he can't. The world is waiting for him on the other side and the distance he must climb is less than it has ever been before.

Chapter 51

Take a second at look at people, I found some gold when I was not looking.

Human Value

10/19/2000

I went to Landover, Maryland for the day and on my way back to Baltimore Airport I got lost, as usual.

Now I have been lost in many places in many towns so it is a situation that I am well acquainted with.

I normally try to pick an upstanding looking person to ask for directions and usually it turns out fine.

I did worry one time in Omaha when I stopped to ask a guy for help and it turned out the shirt he was wearing was not a shirt but body tattoos and that with his shaved head made him look very formidable. But I was already committed to asking and he turned out to be a very nice, helpful guy.

I was in Landover trying to find my way to the Beltway and I pulled into a gas station and thought I was asking one of the attendants for directions. As he got closer I realized that he was not an attendant and by the looks of him had not had an easy life, and looked downright terrible. But again I was committed and I asked for directions and he gave them to me. As I thanked him and was about to ride off he started telling me that he was homeless and in trouble, I waved him to stop talking, pulled out some bills to give him a dollar and a sudden thought ripped through my mind.

I had been having a really good day and this guy was in trouble, even if he was not telling me the truth I could tell that he had been having a very hard time. So instead of waving him off or giving him a buck, he was nice enough to give me directions, I gave him twenty dollars. The look of gratefulness in his eyes was touching, and I left him not only feeling good because he could get some food, but because my act had actually meant something to him.

Twenty dollars is not going to change my life but it probably meant he had a decent dinner for the first time in a while. Many of us have things so good that we forget what it takes to make someone else feel better. Sometimes treating someone else as a "human being" instead of "homeless" is enough, and other times it takes much more.

Everyone has value, especially when they know where you are going and you don't and you really need a restroom.

NOTES

Chapter 52

At least try to be fair.

Let Them Do It Right

6/3/2001

I got into a small fight with my wife the other night.

Every autumn for the last ten years I have been in charge of the Ushers for our High Holy Day Services. These Jewish holidays consist of two twenty-four hour periods-spaced eight days apart. There are usually 6–8 separate services going on during these day long holidays and at an average of five ushers per service means I have to fill about 90 positions to insure that they go smoothly, quietly and run as efficiently as possible. There is often a lot of pressure involved because we also double as helpers to security for things such as bomb scares and, depending on what is happening in the Middle East, possibly even terrorist attacks.

I take being an usher very seriously, which is one reason why I am in charge, and when people ask me to work special events, again I take it as a big deal. Last weekend a close friend's eldest son was being Bar Mitzvahed and they asked me to usher. Of course I agreed and planned to be at the service forty-five minutes before it began, just in case something needed to be done, people came early or our friends needed some help. When my wonderful wife asked me when I was leaving and found out it was earlier then planned she got upset because she wanted to ride with me and take only one car. I told her I needed the time to insure that all was ready for the event and she said it wasn't necessary because nothing should be needed and nothing should go wrong. A small "discussion" followed where she finally said she would take her own car and go when she wanted and I said okay. As it turned out, she did ride with me and went earlier than she had planned and I was needed early at the Bar Mitzvah so it was fortunate that we left when we did.

When I first started working for my father, I did not like to stay past 5:00PM. To be truthful, after everyone had left the building it was a bit intimidating, especially as it got dark. My dad thought I was crazy. The problem continued until I realized the reason. I did not like to stay late, I still don't usually go past 6:00 but I solved the work hours problem by getting in earlier so that I would have the time to get things done the way that I wanted.

Nothing drives me crazier than having to try to condense 2 hours worth of work into one. It condemns you to mediocrity in productivity, loss of energy and momentum and eventual failure. If it takes you two hours to get ready for an 8:00AM meeting then you had better plan to get up early enough to be ready. Not having time is not an excuse for being unprepared or for doing things improperly.

When people tell me they did not have time to get something done I ask them how much sleep they got the night before and where they spent their time after work. Often it is not a case of non-dedication but more a case of inefficiency in time management. I am in the office by 5:00AM and leave between 5 and 6:00PM.

During that time I work, eat, work-out, hopefully get a nap and accomplish what I have to, if not, there is always the weekend. With all that I still have time to see my wife and kids before I go to sleep at 9:30PM.

It is unfair to pressure someone to finish a task if they are working at their maximum efficiency. It is your fault for either not giving them enough time to do the job or misjudging how long it should take. It is also unfair to misuse your own time and then blame everyone else but yourself because you did not finish or did a job halfway.

People are not machines, pack animals or slaves, once they find out they don't have the time or resources to do their best they will begin to lose hope, heart and zest for the job. If you are incredibly lucky they will rise to the occasion and jump levels in their ability to perform. If this happens, be ready to compensate them for their increase in productivity or they will retreat to where they came, or worse, leave for another job. You are killing any hope of you own success by not enabling them to succeed. This doesn't mean that everyone should be able to finish every job they have in order at there own speed. It means that, at the very least, given the situation, if the person works full out then they should be able to do the job to the satisfaction to whoever assigned it. If that is the case than the person who assigns it should have the good sense and faith in their own judgement, and the people under them, to let them do their job and stay out of their way.

It comes down to a matter of faith and believing that other people can do the work beside yourself. Whether it is ushering, writing a report or launching a new product, when you have people there to help you, you have to let them do their jobs, so that you can do yours.

Chapter 53

A stopping in time, an oasis for our minds, a place where we can smile, if only for an instant.

Al's Pond

12/24/2001

We have a stream running past our plant, I was originally afraid of having it there because of flooding. But as times gone on it has yielded a joy that none of us could have anticipated. One bright fall day, my second in command Alice, a/k/a "Al" was outside by the stream and came running in to report that, swimming, right near our front door, was a flock of ducks.

Although the day was busy and hectic, one by one we all made time to go out and watch the birds, cavorting happily in the water, splashing, playing, talking and swimming without seemingly a care in the world. Somehow it added calmness to an otherwise crazy, albeit good day.

From that time forward Al would often goes out to the water during a break and watch for the ducks, and in time I found myself doing the same thing. It is calming, to not only watch them, but search if they are not there, wondering where they have been and toward what destination they are headed. I christened the lookout area "Al's pond."

I belong to a Minyan group that meets on Saturday Mornings. In the Jewish Religion, you need ten people in order to be able to pray as a group and we all meet at our Temple once a week. We run the service ourselves and always during that time there is a portion where we offer our hope that those who are sick will get better. In fact we actually name the individuals that we want to help.

Over the years, prayers were normally offered one person or families and amazingly enough; often the people we asked to be helped actually had some type of improvement. But over the last two years with the many problems in Israel and then our own tragedy with the World Trade Center and the Pentagon we have found ourselves expanding our thoughts for larger groups of people.

We pray for the people in our armed forces, those who helped at the World Trade Center site and of course the victims themselves. We also hope that the world situation will improve, where fear can be reduced and peace once again has a chance to shine.

It often seems insurmountable, we have gone from praying for twenty people to a whole world and yet I know the number does not matter because their fates are not sealed and we can make a change. I know things can be better, even when it feels like everything is melting down. I know this for a fact, when I can gaze into the smile of my daughter, or watch the people marching in a Memorial Day parade. I am sure of it as I watch the faces of my friends in the

Minyan group who, week after week keep praying in the face of seemingly impossible odds and occasionally go across the grain of fate and pull out a miracle and someone gets well.

There will always be "pocket's of goodness and impossible good things that happen even when the whole world seem to be falling around. It is often the little things that keep us going and spur us to do more like watching the winter turn to spring or take a quick walk to Al's pond.

Do bosses make too much money?

Do you love your life?

Chapter 54

Is it worth it? Yes.

Diary of a Business Trip.

Before 9/11/2001

Newark to Denver and back to Newark in one day

Why am I going? There was a buyer change with one of my customers and I wanted to meet her as quickly as possible to try to secure and increase the business we had while at the same time try and make sure that the contacts with the changing buyer remain strong and productive for the future.

Advantages:

Newark to Denver is a direct flight which means, that although it is a long way, I can go and come back in one long day. Therefore, I don't have to tell my kids I won't be home that night and see their sad expressions of missing me.

The weather is supposed to be spring-like so I do not have to take an overcoat or any other luggage and can travel very lightly.

Since the trip is more than two hours, I travel first class or my back could end up like a pretzel. Also, if the flight were delayed I would much prefer to wait it out in the front of the plane.

Disadvantages:

I will be on the go from the time I get up: 3:30AM until I get back home which will probably be about 11:00 that night. I scheduled it for a Friday so I could sleep in on the weekend.

In order to prepare for the trip I did the following: Since I like to work out everyday and there was no time to do so before the plane took-off I worked out twice on the Thursday before. Also, since I don't like a lot of the food on planes I packed enough for the day that I would carry with me. Because I like to work while flying, I carry my laptop with two additional back-up batteries so I won't run out of power.

I print out everything that I can think of for my staff so they are prepared as possible to run the office while I am away.

All this accomplished here is how it went:

3:30AM	*Got up.*
4:40AM	*Got to my office.*
4:50AM	*Cleaned up the parking lot-I don't like garbage.*
5:00AM	*Worked on making sure all of the paperwork for the day was ready until I left for the airport.*
5:40AM	*Left for the airport.*
5:50AM	*Arrived at the airport-it is close by.*

6:45AM *Boarded plane.*

6:10AM *We took off on time. Worked, ate and slept on the plane. Guy was snoring behind me.*

8:15AM *Landed: Mountain time 20 minutes early-what a treat. Everyone on the plane was nice, good trip.*

8:20AM *Called the office-spent ½ hour on the phone and then found out there was a traffic accident that knocked out the power to our town, my office was in darkness and our phones were down. When people called they got no answer—a disaster for a service business like ours. I tried to switch the phone system to different phone lines via call forwarding but it didn't work. I moved my crew into tasks that didn't need power, lights or computers and hope for the best. I am now running late and move to get my rental car waiting for me.*

9:50AM *Got rental car and directions: Always need directions because I always get lost. Trip should take 40 minutes, I figure one hour.*

10:40AM *Got to my customers. Only one wrong turn, which cost me less than five minutes, I will not get cocky. Called some contacts from the lobby and then the people I primarily went to see. Everything went well on the call as did lunch—I took out 2 people. The day was already worth while.*

1:00PM *Back in the waiting room and made more phone calls until 1:30.*

2:30PM *Went back to the airport, gave back my rental, great car.*

2:45PM *My flight was not until 4:45 so I stayed at the airport, wrote, worked and ate some of my food. The office went back on line about 2:00 eastern time and everything seemed to turn out okay. I have one person coming in Saturday at 9:00AM to help me get out a rush job for Monday.*

Airports can be strange places, I watch the people go by, you can tell the seasoned travelers. The thrill of traveling especially at the end of the day has been beaten out of them. They are tired and look fed up with the prospect of flying for business. But the money is where the customers are and you have to attend or someone else will. Every time I get to the point where I am so tired, usually with a headache, that I wonder if it's worth it, I think back and know that much of the largest most profitable pieces of business and customers we have started or increased through trips like this. There is no choice, I will keep going and center on the good.

I fall asleep as I write, drifting in and out of consciousness, hoping to get home soon, to my own bathroom, bathtub and bed. My eldest son said he would wait up for me, a great kid, happily I realize it and know how lucky I am.

3:35PM *Mountain time, 5:35PM at home, I am close to dinner time so I eat some more, besides it lightens my carrying load. There is so much junk food in this airport, and it all tastes so good but I have to resist, stay on my regimen, stay on my schedule continue towards more success.*

The airport television system is too loud, my head still hurts, this is a lonely place.

I have to be careful not to get crumbs in my laptop-last sandwich is now gone, on to the apple and granola bars and if I am really wild I may go for the brownie, ah, the wild side.

3:40PM *Almost an hour before takeoff, I can almost check in, one more step closer to being on the plane.*

We developed a new type of shielding material for the telecommunications industry last week. Actually it was an amazing thing, our customer was in trouble, they called us, we talked about the problem, we created a new material of aluminum and conductive copper, printed it, formed parts and it worked. Sometimes it just works out, parts from nothing within 24 hours. It is great when it works. In addition most of the industry should have use for the material so it opens a new niche area, now to exploit it, market it like crazy and expand to more areas.

3:47PM *I am checked in—yeah! The two granola bars were good.*

4:15PM *I am on the plane*

4:45PM *The plane takes off on time*

I read, sleep, eat my apple brownie and I write. From the nap, my mind is suddenly clear and I am once again thinking rationally optimistically, towards the future.

7:40PM *eastern standard time, I have re-set my clock for home, 2 ½ hours to go and I go back to work. My book about selling should be off press and ready to sell by 1/1/99 along with the first newsletter. The safari hats, you know the kind with the flap down the back are being made in Hong Kong and will also be marketed at the same time. The back flap has a cartoon picture of me and we are selling them with the motto, let me help keep the world off your back or at least off your neck. We are planning to only sell through our WEBSITE and I am already planning to give speeches, interviews on radio and hopefully television and have night courses based on the book. My next book is about relationships called "How to Find and Keep a Suitable Woman or Shut up I Know What's Best For You" should be ready for press in January and will be marketed the same way as the book on sales. All materials moving towards increasing the name recognition of my company our motto and* *myself that quality above all will drive our success and propel our profits. I told you I was feeling optimistic again, amazing what a nap will do.*

8:50PM *My second battery is low, I think I am done writing for the night.*

8:55PM *I changed my mind and keep writing until 9:30*

9:45PM *The plane lands early-another great flight*

The car service is on time to pick me up and I get my car at the office and am back home at 10:45. My eldest son and my wife stay up to see me, life is good and I am ready to do it again.

Do you love your work?

____

____

____

____

____

____

____

____

Are you content?

____

____

____

____

____

____

____

____

____

____

Chapter 55

Don't feel sorry for them because they lost their jobs. Do them a real service by helping them find another.

Empathy—Yes!

12/30/2000

My son came to tell me that he had broken up with his girlfriend. He was in agony because he was her first boyfriend, they are both fourteen years old and he did not want to hurt her. However he also did not want to keep going if his heart was not in it. Imagine, a fourteen-year-old actually considering the thoughts of someone else to the extent that he put himself into a state of gloom.

There are two very different sets of emotions that most people deal with, one is sympathy and the other is empathy. Sympathy is actually a pretty useless emotion. All it means is that you feel sorry that something has happened to someone else and there is nothing that you can do about it except feel sad. This feeling, while appreciated by the other person produces no other positive act.

Empathy, on the other hand is an entirely different emotion. Instead of reactive it is highly active. To be empathetic means that you have to be able to define a situation, it's participants and the possible, intended, and the actual results. By being empathetic you not only show that you understand all of the components of the situation but that you have thought of ways that you can personally help and if all else fails then the very least is to commiserate on the bad twists of fate.

Being empathetic is an absolutely crucial ability to have when you are trying to market and sell yourself. Since we do not live in a vacuum everything that happens to everyone else affects us and vise-versa. Therefore if you are trying to sell someone who just got a new promotion or was passed over you will have to react very differently as various situations come up.

Here is an example, one of our customers is a very large telecommunications firm, and like most others their stock price has plummeted in the past year. Like most companies their employee benefit plan is normally packed with the stock of the company. Therefore when the stock price tanked last year so did a lot of value in most employees retirement accounts. What does this mean? It means that in many of the conversations that I have with employees of that company the price of the stock is going to come up. That price affects their money and their lives, which means it affects the way that they conduct business.

It is your responsibility if you are an empathetic person to know about the company, the stock, what it has done in the past day and week and how it affects the people you are dealing with.

As time marches on, the economy is always paramount in the minds of the employees of the company. Your viewpoints as to marketing yourself and your company have to be directly proportional as to what is happening.

Remember, what is the most important thing to a buyer, or anyone else? The answer is their job, the second most important thing is a better job. The next most important thing is their financial well bring and their future. After that, comes the health of their family, the state of their marriage and any other thing they are willing to share with you. You want to know as much about everything as you can so that you will be able to read them as well as possible. You want to have an overall view of their lives so that you can affect change in a positive way that will benefit you and them at the same time.

You may say to yourself that you are only one person and what can you possibly do to change the course of a large corporation and the answer is plenty. First of all you don't have to change the whole company just help the people you are directly dealing with. That help can range from feeding them information about what is happening in other parts of the corporation, to job possibilities within and outside the company. One person or piece of business at a time, not with corporate takeovers, just changing one life for the better.

Aggressiveness is wonderful and never giving up is great, but not having the ability to empathize with the people you are dealing with can make the difference as to whether you make it at all or are a superstar bringing in millions in commissions. Your future is in your ability to be able to understand the people around you, both with your customers and throughout your world so you can work with the potential that is there instead of wasting your times on stuff that can never be. Empathy will give you the clear picture as to what is possible so you don't have to rush blindly in all directions. It also gives you the ability to pick your attacks and refine your strategy so it doesn't even look like you are in battle.

The only bad thing is that since you can see what the results of your actions, you know when your decisions might indirectly hurt other people and even though you know it has to be done, you often feel more pain than the recipients themselves. My son has this ability and there is nothing I can do to help him. It is another trade-off of life, in order to see the paths to greatness you also see the results of your journey.

Chapter 56

If you are not in top physical, emotional, and financial shape they you will be beaten by someone who is.

Fat and Happy is an Oxymoron

11/7/2000

So you have made it, you are now successful in whatever definition it means to you.

Maybe you had you heart set on marrying one person since the time you were five years old but there were was one problem. You were overweight and that person could not consider anyone with that characteristic. So you trained and dieted for years until finally on your twenty-fifth birthday you were a prize human specimen in perfect physical form. Your abs were solid your backside tight, you skin was clear and you looked the best you ever could.

The other person looked at you in and fell madly in love and you got married. On your wedding night you realized that you had attained your dream and knew you did not have to worry about watching yourself any more. You "had" the other person, they were committed for life and as far as you were concerned it did not matter what happened because you had that wedding ring.

So you stopped training and as the years passed you became fat and happy. The only problem was your partner married the thin version of you not the fat facsimile. The drive and determination that had made you became what she loved had been dissipated into a wake of cake infested dementia. The happier (fatter) you got the more angry your partner became because there was nothing she could do to stop your slide into oblivion so she went her own way, and if you were lucky you got to stay for the ride even if it was on the sidelines.

It is the same thing in business. Do you know what I think of when I see competitors who have made it and are very happy, contented and love to talk about their previous triumphs? I think of opportunity and that they are now vulnerable. I am like a shark perfectly happy to take little bites wherever I can. Those small jobs that are a pain in the neck to my competitors, the kind where you don't make any money and have to work nights and weekends. The jobs that make you very exposed to triumph or disaster. People who are fat and happy do not want to rock the boat or take chances and they are people I love to be around because they mean opportunity.

It is very difficult to fight against strong willed, driven directed people who have specific goals in mind. Why do you think large corporations are always buying small entrepreneurs and their companies? Not only for their technology, they are also making sure that the small company owner becomes an ally instead of a threat. They absorb the owner with the hope that their drive will infuse the larger company or at the very least negate the threat to their existence. Of course the larger company doesn't have any idea that the smaller upstart is bent on taking them over from the inside but that is a different story.

If you are unfortunate enough to have a mate who has given up trying to maximize their mental, physical and intellectual structure because they are contented with the way things are, then your choices are the same as in business.

You can try and re energize them, keep and accept them as they are, or leave. If you are happy and contented where you are than the odds are good that someone like me is watching you, ready to start nipping at your heels with the intent of devouring you later. Whatever got you to your successful position is still there someway deep inside, bring it out soon, retire or get used to the idea of calling someone else boss.

How long do you plan to stay in your current job?

- ☐ ***1 year***
- ☐ ***5 years***
- ☐ ***Indefinitely***

I like to think about myself because:

____

____

____

____

____

____

____

____

____

____

____

____

____

____

Chapter 57

You are a force of one, in command of your internal forces, with the ability to change the world. Your fear is your ticket to freedom and everything else you want.

Fear is Good

When I was growing up I was afraid. I was scared of bigger kids, grown-ups, strangers, doing badly in school and almost everything else you could think of. I hated being afraid, that feeling in my stomach that I would "just take it" in whatever form the abuse might take. I would be left later with the horrible feeling of inadequacy and wishing a chance for a do-over. In my mind I would always reconstruct those situations where I felt I had not acted with the right amount of courage or forcefulness and in retrospect the correct action always seemed so clear that I cried for not having done it right the fist time.

As I got older, I came to understand some very important facts that have kept me in good company over the last twenty years. The fact that I did not like to go onto dark unlit streets, walk past groups of older kids, or get into potential bad situations did not mean I was scared, it meant that I was being careful and smart. Being scared was not a reaction out of cowardice, it was more a reaction to bad judgement for getting into the wrong situations in the first place.

The other thing I learned was that if I was ready to fight then I probably would not have to. In my case that meant training in various types of martial arts for years that gave me the physical confidence and mental toughness to feel, while not totally secure, a lot calmer so my fear level was greatly reduced.

I am going to fly in two weeks, the first time since the World Trade Centers went down, and I am a little concerned. I am flying to Omaha, Nebraska. While that might seem a safe place, it is the location of one of the biggest defense installations in the country, and I am flying on December 7th, the anniversary of the bombing of Pearl Harbor. I know the statistics are with me and the odds are greatly in my favor that I would have a better chance to be hit by a car then blown in up in a plane, but I still think about it.

Fear is something that never goes away, but it doesn't necessarily have to be a bad thing. I feel fear when I am unprepared, not ready for what is coming. Of course you can't be ready for a bombing but you can train for many other situations, both mental and physical.

We live in difficult times, the economy is still moving downward and many people are losing their jobs. A big part of my job, besides running our company is selling. I am supposed to sell millions of dollars worth of labels, tags plastic and metal parts to companies mostly within the United States. But how can I do it when not many people want to buy? How can I go on when most people I talk to, are more concerned about losing their jobs than what I am trying to sell? How can I keep going when many of the people I have known for years have either been fired, early retired, laid off or their companies have gone out of business or merged with others?

There will always be tough times and there will still always be people who are ready to buy. My job is to find those people, and using anything as an excuse for not succeeding is just that, an excuse.

Business runs by the odds, if you call 100 people looking for customers then, if you are competent, at least 2 or 3 will have an interest and maybe one will be ready to buy something. Make enough phone calls, and it might take thousands, and you will have the basis for a new group of customers who can either start you on your career, build up what you have already created or replace older accounts that are failing.

That fear in your stomach is not your enemy, it is your best friend, your permanent alarm clock to remind you that you have to keep pushing and attacking to go after what you want and keep focused on the long term goals. Nothing means anything, world events do not matter, stay focused on your goal of getting business, make your calls in a competent manner and you will get customers. If the fear becomes overwhelming and you can't force yourself to keep going then, either quit, or find an additional outlet where you can become stronger, like in your body.

Strength in any part of your life will raise the level of your energy across the board and enable you to keep going in the toughest areas. You are at war with yourself, you have to train your mind, body and soul to do what has to be done to achieve what you said you wanted. That outcome will be a direct result of how well you can maintain, direct and increase your interior forces. You are in for the fight of your life and how well you do will determine your success rate in all areas and help to keep your stress level to within acceptable limits. Don't blame your lack of success on what is happening in the world, it is all your responsibility. Rejoice in this fact because it is the one place where you can affect the biggest rate of change and improvement.

Chapter 58

You want this? Then do that.

Money is a Tool

8/5/2000

I was in Hong Kong a few years ago.

What is Hong Kong? A small rock in a vast ocean. It has virtually no natural resources except a port and everything has to be transported on and off the island. How did it become one of the great financial centers of the world?

Money is a tool.

I was just in Bermuda. What is Bermuda? A small rock in a vast ocean. Again why does it exist? It has no natural resources except a port, it doesn't even have a fresh water supply of its own, it has to rely on rain water. Tourism, though very important, is not it most important area of business, it is re-insurance.

Why does Hong Kong, Bermuda, Taiwan and a bunch of others like it exist? It is not their abundance of natural resources, it is because of their location and a group of people decided that it was in their best interest to create these centers to allow them to do business in an easier, more efficient more profitable way.

On a local level when I hear people talk about money I hear them say that they want a "lot" of it whatever that means. They want enough for retirement and they watch it like a hawk when they do or don't spend it. I think that most people miss the true value and force of their money.

The real secret and benefit of money lies in its ability to influence others to do what is in your best interest and hopefully theirs.

I pay the people in our company well. Why do I do it? If I can maximize the amount of energy and productivity I can get from my people then it will enable me to keep and train less people. It enables me to be able to train them longer and to higher levels and make much better use of them. In return for giving me every ounce of energy they have during the day I enter into a contract with them where I will pay them well, have a work environment that is productive, cheerful, and fun, and most importantly treat them with the respect and understanding that their energy output deserves.

Everyone in my company has a brain and an opinion. During our morning meetings I listen to whatever anyone has to say. I got some of the best business advice from my head of shipping. He mentioned one day that he thought that I was branching out into to many business areas at one time and we were going to spread our resources too thin. I took his advice to heart and after a great deal of thought decided that he was right and I streamlined our operation and refocused on our best areas for growth and profits.

Often you are best off if you listen to the people who are actually doing the work. They are closest to what is happening, and it is their opinion that should be solicited before future actions take place.

Money is the tool that allows you to access the brains of the people in your company who can often save you a fortune in time and energy. If you believe that people should just be happy that they have a job or that they should do things for the good of the company you are kidding yourself. The responsibility for your operation and your people rests solely with those above them. If you do not allow them to benefit from the fruits of their labors by paying them well and giving them a good working environment then you have violated the contract of taking care of each other that is so vital to be being able to grow quickly and efficiently.

What about your home life? Do you listen to your kids? After all, they are a mixture of hopefully the best of their parents and relatives. They can have incredibly fast minds that have not been hampered by a lifetime of experience that can retard the flow of inspiration and deep thought. Do you pay them allowance? Do you pay them to do chores? Are they motivated by money? One of the greatest things you can do for a child is allow them the joy of doing a job, getting paid for it and then getting the reward by spending the money. An additional joy is that of learning to save for the future towards a big event that they can directly influence positively by their actions.

I have a nephew, you should have seen his attitude about money and work change as soon as he realized that he wanted a car and the only way he was going to get it was to get a job.

He came to work for me and you will never see a more motivated kid. It is a joy to watch him soak in the knowledge necessary to do his job and he doesn't even realize he is learning.

We have so many chances both through business and personally to positively influence those around us. In many cases they need the motivation and money can be the tool that you use to get that contract going between the two of you.

I have another nephew who wants to buy a computer. After he started working for me for a few months I saw him at a family function and the garbage needed to be taken out. Without thinking I told him to please take out the garbage and he stopped what he was doing and took it out immediately. His mother looked at me and I apologized for ordering her son, she smiled and said I could do it anytime. The problem was that until he was working for me and the contract established I could never have told him to do it. Once it was established there is not limit to the growth potential and production possible, as long as the person on the receiving end is getting compensated well in their eyes.

You will pay "x" to get "Y" done, and if they do extra, then "z" will happen. We happily live in a capitalistic society and it is based on money, but you can modify that equation to your own advantage by allowing people to maximize their capabilities for themselves, and then everyone wins.

NOTES

CHAPTER 59

My Dad was right: excuses are worth nothing.

I Am Tired

7/7/2000

I am tired, I am so tired that my body hurts. I pulled my back playing tennis yesterday and I just found out we did not a get a giant piece of business because someone found a better way to fix a customer problem than we did. I do not like to lose, I do not like to even admit I am tired and it is times like these that I remember what my father taught me. He said one out of twenty.

For every twenty pieces of business I went after, I would be fortunate to get one.

If you are expecting an easy time at trying to get people to buy whatever you are selling, whether it is yourself, your company or your products then you might as well give up now. It is a long, hard war against the best, most prepared people in the world. Whether it is a pastor with his congregation, a President with his country or a salesman selling computers the best are the ones who are able to sell the most i.e. have the biggest congregations, the richest country and sell the best computers. Remember the fourth rule of selling: if you are not 100% dedicated to what you are doing and even ready to die for your beliefs then you will be beaten on a percentage basis by those who will.

Sounds hoaky does it? That much commitment to your job, that kind of belief in what you are doing? On the contrary, what you do for a living is the defining area of your life. Describe yourself, and the odds are good you will start by describing your job and where you work. We are all programmed to judge our self worth by our careers. You are dedicated to it whether you realize it or not and it is that measure of commitment which will ultimately decide your slice of the success pie.

The people you are fighting against, and I mean fighting, have the experience to get, hold onto and expand the business you have. They also have the knowledge to ward off the attacks by people like you and me. Business is taken, you will take accounts from someone and they will take them from you, you are fighting against people who believe that their self worth is based on how much and how well they sell so they will use every asset available to them to keep you out. No matter what area or what business, if you are not prepared to go all out through all of your life than you will gradually lose to those who are.

This is not meant to discourage you from trying, on the contrary, it is one of the few definite things in life. By knowing your parameters it is much easier to understand the commitment of time, resources and interior guts needed to launch your own attacks. By knowing you cannot expect to be successful more than one out of twenty, you will not be destroyed when you don't sell the first fifteen people you meet. You will not have unreal expectations and looked on as a failure by your interior soul.

I lost that big piece of business because I was ready to supply an on-time product that was of superior quality to my competition. The product of the other company was not as good and might mess-up their machinery when in long term use. There is a possibility that a major breakdown could occur and completely screw up and stop their operations. But the cost of my product was more then the other company, and the customer decided that they would make the other product work regardless of modifications, time lost or repairs they would have to go through.

I am not happy about not getting the business, I spent a lot of time and money on testing and prototypes but I have already moved onto other projects. I did not get this project because of money, I could not get the next one because of a new technology. It will happen again, probably another 19 times before we get another big piece of business or a new customer. But it doesn't matter because I know that the one out of twenty rule will insure that our company will continue to grow. I also know that as long as our commitment as a company and my commitment to myself and others remains absolute then that too will insure the successes for us all.

The world is now one place, the only thing that separates one person or company from another is their commitment to service their customers in every way possible and understand that you only win by the percentages and not on the specifics.

You are out their to sell yourself, your company and your products, it has to be a defined, tactically planned journey in order to utilize all of your resources to their fullest extent. Remember you are fighting people like me, don't have unreal expectations at any point in your life and you have the chance to not only make as good a living as you want, but have a great time doing it.

And now it is time to take my tired body and go back to work.

Chapter 60

Do not underestimate your ability to influence, support, and help.

In Support of the Rite of Passage

In the Jewish religion there is no greater trial by fire then becoming a Bar or Bat Mitzvah. This rite of passage involves studying for years leading up to your thirteenth birthday. Long in advance you get the date and all life leads up to that one defining moment when you are standing in front your family, friends and the heads of the temple and go through a litany of various prayers and readings in both English and Hebrew. The hardest part of the service is reading from the Torah, which is the basic text for Jewish law and history. You have to read the passage in Hebrew, without the benefit of vowels, and it is extremely difficult, especially in front of everyone who is important to you.

David is a good friend of my middle son Alex. He is a really good kid with a big heart who is not a scholar but tries very hard. I remember about a year ago when my son was having a bad day and he decided not to go to a school dance scheduled for that night. He was feeling miserable and kept refusing to go even after his friend repeatedly called him. Finally, David gave up and Alex retired to watch TV for the night, depressed and miserable. Suddenly there was a knock at our front door and it was his friend, he had decided to take matters into his own hands and had asked his dad to drive him over and try to get Alex to go. Needless to say, this extraordinary display of friendship and caring did the trick. Alex got dressed, went to the dance and had a great time.

It was not the first time that David had displayed this type of caring, so it was with this in mind that I watched him this morning. It was his turn to take this rite of passage on his journey to becoming an adult, it was his time to become a Bar Mitzvah and the moment in the service was fast approaching for him to read his Torah potion. Under extreme pressure before, this was the toughest part and I could see the stress level skyrocketing on his face. He was looking around trying to marshal his interior forces and I realized he could use some help.

I believe that you can transfer energy between two beings, I believe that physical contact is the most efficient vehicle, but the energy can also be delivered via mental concentration. That energy can not only make someone feel better but help them with an extra touch of cosmic force to get through whatever they are facing. I had never actually formally tried it before and I was hoping it might have an effect, I owed it to David to try for helping my son.

I started to stare at him, even though he was not looking at me and keep concentrating and sending positive, supporting thoughts and as I felt my energy level peaking he looked at me and instantly knew what I was trying to do. The stress on his face vanished, replaced by firm resolve and in the next instant he was up, reading his portion and doing a phenomenal job. The rest of the service was a breeze for him and he finished in triumph.

Later in the day at the reception I went up to him and asked if he could feel what I was trying to do and miraculously he said he did. The transfer had happened and I was able to actually help someone with sending out positive energy from my mind.

Was the world changed? Of course not, a miracle had not occurred, but something very important did happen on a smaller scale. We are taught that there are all kinds of limits in terms of space and time. We are structured from birth within certain borders as to what can be accomplished, and even worse what should be attempted. If we accept those limits, where we allow ourselves to venture, how much have we preordained ourselves to mediocrity? How can we have any hope of gigantic achievement if we limit ourselves before we begin?

We are all born with interior energy, of which we are the definers for where it is used. Utilizing that life force and all of your interior resources will define how well you do in all areas. If you are fortunate, you might actually have the chance to directly benefit someone else by sharing your own energy to help them through one of their defining moments in life and becoming a part of that moment yourself. My son is lucky to have a friend like David, and it was an honor for me to be there to help him, even in the small way that I did, especially from across the room.

I like to think about the world because:

____

____

____

____

____

____

____

____

____

____

____

____

____

____

Chapter 61

I like to be nice. It pays to be positive.

Being Positive is Hard Work

7/2/2000

When I was growing up I always wondered about the people who were not nice. Those who would shoot off their mouths to mock others, belittle them to increase their own limited self worth, degrade others in order to rise in the estimation of their mini minded peers.

I tried not to play that game, because to be truthful, I knew how cruel their comments could be , how they could rip right through you and make you feel inadequate, lowly and worth nothing and I did not want to be like them. As I went into high school I learned that I had the ability to throw out these types of negative comments whenever I was attacked. It got to the point that I knew that I could destroy anyone verbally if I just let mind go with my initial reactions. I saw how much it could hurt and dedicated myself to the ideal that I would take as much as possible before I would unleash my own torrent of abuse. With my martial arts training, and the quick verbal ability that I developed, there were few situations that I could not handle.

But I asked myself why? Why should I have had to enhance my ability to physically and mentally destroy people, why did I have to protect myself from people who pounced on anyone they thought were any weaker in any area? Why do we as humans feel it is our right to bring ourselves up while putting others down? Why do we hope for the destruction of others and use it as a basis to make ourselves feel better?

Our neighbor does not get a promotion and we are secretly glad. Another's business goes bankrupt and we are happy because he tried to be "better" then the rest of us. We judge ourselves by the misery of others, at least that is what a lot of people do because it is easier than blaming ourselves.

Being negative in every way is easier than being positive. When most people view a situation, they always look at it from the negative viewpoint first and then to see if they can personally benefit from it. That is why our television news programs love fires and explosions and why we study wars and battles in school. Think back, how much time in your life has been spent studying the positive aspects of any situation, how much do we focus on what is good? The answer is that we don't because it is harder. As human beings it is easy for us to be negative, being positive takes a lot more energy and most people don't want to expend the effort or worse yet do not know how.

It is a great effort to get up in the morning and focus on the good, what is peaceful and positive. To focus on what we need to do to make our lives better for ourselves, the people around us and the world as a whole.

What does this have to do with self promotion and making money? Everything. Think about the people you want around you. You don't want to be with depressed people, you want the ones who smile and make you feel good. You want to be around those who are having fun, making money in an honest way, bringing things towards positive conclusions because you hope it might rub off. You want them to bring you along for the ride, because their positive view might rub off on you.

People like to be around me, because I smile, say good morning and try lift their spirits, help them to increase their positive energy for the whole day. I talk to people on the phone all day and one of my purposes in life is to bring them up and make them happier. In exchange, they are happy to hear from me and sometimes even business results. It is wonderful for everybody because one you send out positive energy it often comes back to reenergize you once you are tired. I love to make a positive difference.

If you walk into our offices you are going to see a lot of happy, yelling people, moving quickly, talking and processing orders and working towards a common goal of a more productive business. It is not just the good wages they get but is also the place where they work. It is wild atmosphere of fun, purpose and building something good. Everyone in our office knows they count, their opinions matter and they are all taken seriously. We are in business and in life together and they know it.

When I am at home, again you can hear the laughter, the joy of a family growing and being happy and doing lots of yelling and getting things done.

The world can be a wonderful place and you can get a great deal done if you have the right attitude. The people you love, and your customers, want to be around someone positive, growing and being successful. Don't think that you can be depressing and negative and things will go well because they can't. Life takes a major effort, and since you have to participate in it anyway, you might as well have the best time possible. Being "up" is your best chance at being successful in all areas, if you doubt it look around you and see who is having the most fun.

CHAPTER 62

I you don't know "the code" then it is much harder to win.

The Code

8/20/2001

When I was in Junior High there was a group of students from the "Valley" The Valley was a working class neighborhood full of tough kids who hung out together. I was not from there, I was part of the middle class area on the other side of town and the two groups generally kept separated, unless united by a common area like sports.

Gym class had no class boundaries and I found myself in one dominated by the kids from the Valley. I was as scared of them like everyone else but I was taking martial arts which helped to level the playing field.

Sports were taken very seriously in that class and when playing basketball the idea when placing a pick (lure your opponent to slam into one of your teammates while he is not looking) was to inflict as much damage on the "pickee" as possible. I liked a rough game and I liked playing with them, until their leader, a guy named Joe, came after one of my team members who had the ball and I threw a pick on him that sent him sailing. He landed, was hurt and went off limping to the school nurse.

Now, my pick had been a clean maneuver but I had hurt one of "their" guys, especially their leader and I figured that the best I could hope for was only to get beaten up a little in the showers. I knew what I had to do, which was act as if everything was fine, so I went to the locker room, had a shower, got dressed and nothing happened. As I went to class I stopped off at the nurse and there was Joe, with an ice pack on his ankle. He saw me and smiled, I asked if he was okay and he said sure. From that day when we saw each other we nodded and smiled. There was a code, we both knew it and both followed it. I hit him clean, he got hurt and showed no malice, I had showed respect by checking on him at the nurse.

Last weekend I was at the Industrial Design Society Of American Annual Conference in Boston. I was also seeing customers in the area and I was very concerned about driving in a strange city with lots of construction which could mean big headaches. My worst nightmare came true, I got lost and started wandering around the downtown area. Starting to panic I opened my window and asked the man in the car next to me how to get to Park Place. In my crazed state I thought he said I could not get there from here, then true panic set in, I was trapped, destined to never get back to my hotel and miss the seminar I had to give the next morning.

But once again, the code came into play. I knew that, as a guy, if you show the ultimate in despair by actually admitting that your are lost then it will bring out the goodness in strangers. I stopped by some rough looking construction workers, admitted straight out that I was totally lost and one stepped to my car and gave me directions, I thanked him profusely, he smiled and I helped to make his day because he did a good deed. I was back to the hotel in under fifteen minutes.

The code may be unwritten, but it is definitely there and loathe to those who ignore it.

My father-in-law, whom I love and respect dearly, loves to eat dinner at our house but he causes a few problems. One of our house rules is that everyone has to be served before anyone starts. My father in law knows the rule, ignores it, and says it is dumb and he won't follow it. In the process he is insulting my wife, ignoring the house rules, making everyone uncomfortable and setting a bad example for his grandchildren. He knows the code and refuses to follow it.

Every situation has a set of rules attached, whether specifically in sales or generally in life. If you do not know the rules, normally all you have to do is admit it, something that is very tough to do, and people generally will be nice and tell them to you. If they won't, then you do not want to be involved with them anyway, but at least you know where you stand. Ignoring the rules, or worse, trying to bluff your way through or putting your own set to a wrong situation invites disaster and it is your own fault.

When you are trying to sell or satisfy the needs of another to get what you want, the code or rules of the situation must be followed if you are going to have any chance for success. Admit when you are wrong, when you don't know them. Be comfortable saying that you are sorry and the odds are good that your life will move a lot more smoothly. Ignore them at your peril. Just ask my father-in-law, who may be eating alone tonight.

Chapter 63

Consistency and structuring are not boring. They are efficient and are the quickest routes to success.

The Dog and the Chicken

12/27/2001

We had just gone away on vacation and for the first time allowed one of our kids to bring a friend. We originally planned to have all six of us in two rooms but we luckily got a third one at the last minute. I figured my oldest son and his friend would love to bunk together and that seemed to be the case until nightfall when they both decided they wanted to be closer to the family and wanted to move back in with the rest of us.

I don't know about you but I like it quiet when I sleep, I mean really quiet, and the idea of having two kids in the same room with me meant that I was destined for very little rest and a lot of staring at the ceiling. So I asked if anyone would mind if I went to the other room by myself. The other room was not as nice as the two we had, it was more for the staff then the guests. But for me it was just fine, a place to sleep, quiet except for only the noise I chose to make. As an added benefit, my mountain bike got to spend the night indoors instead of outside in the cold.

Everyone seemed surprised that I would choose to be there, being that the room wasn't as nice and that I would be alone. I replied that the peace and quiet was worth more then the decrease in luxury, and that it was a trade I would always take, a situation where the results would always be the same.

"Michael, No!" he said to the dog, "Leave that chicken alone!" As he yelled, and I watched, a golden retriever ran along the side of the road where I was mountain biking, chasing a squawking chicken. "Michael, you know better!" he said as the chicken outran the dog. The owner was still screaming, and the dog, realizing that the jig was up, came slowly back to him with his tail between his legs. The dog dropped at his owner's feet, his master still yelling, then turned onto his back and exposed his stomach in a show of complete surrender. It was a dance that I am sure had happened frequently between the owner, the dog and the same squawking chicken. All knew the outcome before it had begun, but all had to participate in the same way, every time, and given normal circumstances the outcome would always remain the same.

People and life run in patterns. A structure in life not only makes for a more efficient use of time but also reduces the almost unlimited number of decisions that we all have to make every day. What to wear, what to have for lunch, where to go to college; the possibilities are too numerous to contend with, which is why habits are such a great thing. It is also why, when you are selling, you can use these "patterns" to predict the actions of the people you want to deal with in various situations.

Since you know that any buyer's first concern is their job, and that their second biggest concern is getting a better job, you have a decent idea how they will react as to anything new that happens. After being with them for a while, you also know how they will conduct themselves in day to day patterns, so you can tailor your sales approach to make the most of their everyday behavior. I know I must sound like a psychologist talking about a case, but in many ways it is similar because as a salesman, your job is to watch and understand the people you are dealing with. You goal and your passion must be to understand what your customers want and need so that you can fill those requirements, and get what you want in return.

There is nothing diabolical or wrong with using these living patterns to your advantage. On the contrary, you can be of more help to your buyers and the people around you by being able to predict what will happen correctly, on average, and thereby reduce or eliminate the possible areas of strife that would occur had you not headed them off. If you can be the person who can reduce, or even eliminate, these sources of stress and pain for your buyer, or for anyone else in your life, then you will be the person they turn to on an ever increasing basis, and will also be the recipient of all the business they can give.

You want to be the person who comes to mind when trouble starts or something new comes up. To be in that position you have to take the time to learn about the people with whom you are dealing, their patterns and habits, and how you can serve them first so that they can help you in return. As sure as the dog will never get the chicken, and that I will always take the quieter room, you can be sure that the person who studies and understands these types of patterns is destined to achieve the success they deserve.

Chapter 64

Experience is both a master and a servant.

The Ghosts of the Playing Field

12/26/2001

I love to go to Lenox, Massachusetts in the Berkshire Mountains on vacation, it has some of the best mountain biking trails anywhere and I love the challenge of barreling up and down the hills, trying to stay upright while still watching the beautiful countryside go whizzing by me. A few days between Christmas and New Years provided one of those opportunities for me and although it was only about 32°F outside I donned my protective outdoor weather gear and sped off to the hills.

I have a favorite spot that is a few miles from the resort, and as I climbed the last hill to the entrance to the park I noticed that it seemed to be getting colder and darker more rapidly than I had anticipated. It was only about 3:00PM, but it was the dead of winter and it seemed to be turning towards dusk faster that I expected. As I got to the entrance I noticed that the entire trail was full of ice.

I found myself weighing the options. I could go ahead and ride through the woods to one of my favorite views and look at the sunset over the mountains. Afterwards I could ride downward through the trails and then come back upward to the entrance and continue my ride. My other option was to turn around and take an alternate route on a paved road that was probably ice-free. I knew that if I fell on the trail and got hut that I would have a about 15 minutes before I froze to death and even with a cell phone the odds of survival would not be good. I've had this same conversation with myself hundreds of times throughout my life through various types of adventures. Although I was always prepared with the best outdoor clothing, this time I still found myself hesitating.

I remembered the story about the championship fighter who knew it was time to retire when he thought about where to punch someone as opposed to having already done it. Once you start thinking about doing something the time had come to realize that maybe you should not proceed. The thrill and bravado of going forth was being tempered by the chances of getting hurt and possible death and then it hit me. I was no longer thinking like a young man, I had, in an instant moved through the portal to middle age.

Yes, chronologically I was there already, I was almost forty-six years old and although in the best shape of my life, the signs of age, especially in my left knee, were beginning to show. I was no longer willing to risk anything to see a view of the mountains that I could experience another time. Suddenly the thrill of living life at bad odds was not as appealing as being able to maximize my potential in the areas where I was still getting stronger.

I turned around and left the entrance to the park, my head flooded with the thoughts of where my life would go now. Feeling a little depressed I kept cycling, and noticed that it was getting colder quickly, so I put on all the clothes

I was carrying and was still cold. " I must be nuts being out here", I thought to myself. Being out in the freezing cold, even if I was on an ice-free pavement seemed a little crazy. I looked around, there was not another cyclist in site, I was alone and suddenly, epiphany number two hit me.

I was alone on the playing field. All those years growing up when I was overweight and could not keep up with the kids with the wash board stomachs who used to look at me with pity when I tried to compete on their level. The taunts of one of them, about how my stomach fell over my bathing suit, still cut in to me as deeply as when it was first hurled more than thirty years ago. But that guy was not out here, in fact, I think the last time I saw him he had a gut on him that would have hung over his bathing suit. Fact is, most of the people who used to be in good shape had faded away from the athletic scene. As I thought back, I realized that from my youth, I was almost alone in level of fitness that I was in. The people who had mocked me were gone and I was on the playing field alone, I had won.

As I rode on I could almost see the ghosts of my past rising up before me, never to be a force against me again. They were not dead, just human like me, with no great power, either physical or mental which could be used to make me feel like less of a person. Yes I was older but I was also a lot smarter and had used what abilities I had to maximize what I was given. The limitations on any of life's playing fields had been put there by me, and therefore by definition I was the only one who could take them away. Whether it be sports, work, selling or any place where I was involved with other people, the power of where I was positioned would always be dictated by me.

Chapter 65

Our minds have no barriers, our lives no borders, unless we put them there.

Air Tennis

2/6/2002

It was a cold, snowy January day in New Jersey. My wife was gone for a much deserved vacation with her mother and sister, which meant that I went to a Bar Mitzvah of a family friend with only my son Alex. The reception was at a local tennis club and the outdoor courts, without their nets and surrounded by naked trees, looked like a testament to the fact that spring would never come.

When my wife and I go to parties, I am normally the outgoing one, making sure to meet enough people so she has someone to talk to. One of the reasons she likes to go with me is that I love to "work" a room, especially with people I don't know. In this case, since I was solo, and I was under instructions from Alex that I should avoid contact with him in front of his friends, after all he is thirteen, I could do as I wanted.

There were some interesting people, but I needed a break and went to look at the snowy landscape out one of the large window and there I saw an amazing scene. Two boys, my son's age, were playing an imaginary game of tennis in the parking area. One boy would serve and the other would return and the points were ending with an overhead smash by one or the other. It did not seem to matter that is was 29 degrees, snowing, cold and they were not wearing gloves. They were in a fantasy land of their own, in the summer with shorts and tea shirts playing on a court which had hosted the best tennis players in the world of which they were now two.

They were in heaven, for that brief moment in time and they had created that world for themselves. The world they inhabited they had built from scratch constructed only with the tools of their imaginations.

We live in a nice house in a town where I wanted to be since I can remember. As I was growing up I would look at people in Short Hills as successful and powerful who seemed to have the world at their feet. The streets were beautiful and well kept, the downtown looked affluent and the houses were immaculately kept with lawns and gardens that would make a greens keeper proud.

Ten years ago, when I was thirty six years old, my wife and I bought a house there. It is a great place and we just built on a porch, but there is one problem. The front hallway has stained wood floors that have been worn down by time. I have been pushing my wife to have the floors re-sanded and stained, but that would mean taking out all of the furniture and vacating the house for a week due to the dust and fumes. She has been saying there is no need, the floors aren't that bad and I should live with it.

Every night when I come home and drive down my street, I get a thrill. This was my dream to live on a street like this, in a house like I have, but not with the scratched, worn floors in the front hall. A small thing you might say, but it was marring my dream and I was determined to get them re-done. My wife was just as determined that we leave them as they were, and we have been at a stalemate for a year.

Finally she came up with a great idea. Instead of sanding and staining the floors, we could have the areas specially painted with a "faux" print of a walkway. It would have a really "cool" look and would mean we did not have to sand the floors nor have a dust problem. This would localize the work so the all the rooms would not have to be re-done. As soon as I heard the idea I loved it and modified the view in my dream to include the painted floors and then everything was fine.

Dreams are very important, often more than reality because what you want to see can often over shadow what is actually there. To the kids at the tennis club, that court and the summer day were real, even if it was winter with no lines, balls, racquets or heat. To me, the house, my vision will not be complete until the floor are fixed. It does not matter what anyone else thinks, whether it is my dream, those kids or yours, to ignore them is inviting disaster because reality is based on how the individual sees it. People can move mountains if they believe in what can be, but can achieve nothing if they don't see past someone else's reality.

CHAPTER 66

Those who can, do. Those who can't, complain.

I Am Not Stupid

10/26/2000

I am in the midst of trying to rent or buy a building. It would seem like an easy enough process. I have the financing in line, I know the area I want to be, the requirements of the building regarding space, power, roof lightening etc. So why should it be so hard?

Since I had never bought an industrial type building or rented this much space, I had no idea what was in store for me until I started looking. I have never seen a more difficult, nasty, uncaring, self-centered group of people on my life.

It seems that having money and knowing what I want is not enough for these people, I also have to agree with them that everything they say is gospel and I am an idiot. I am supposed to believe them when they tell me not to tell the truth to the town building departments about the amount of parking I need so I can get a permit. Or that the illegal construction in their building is no big deal and why did I tell the town about it in the first place? As the realtor said I "let the cat out of the bag" to the town and it was my fault that my people found out about the illegal construction that the owner did not "happen" to know about.

Do I have a sign with the word painted IDIOT on my forehead? Does the fact that I am a boss and owner of a thriving company automatically make me stupid, unknowing, unworldly or uncaring?

Most people are not bosses or owners and when you are working for someone else you only view them with preconceived ideas. For instance many people feel that bosses love to fire people. Nothing could be further from the truth, I hate to fire anyone. Taking away someone's livelihood, especially when they have a family, is horrible and has cost me many painful hours of impending dread. I detest that they know, without me telling them, that I think that they have failed and they are not good enough to work here. I can't stand looking at their faces when they realize they have to go and I really hate when they react badly and I have even been threatened.

People think it is easy to be the boss, but you have to think about your people, their well being (yes we do think about that) the well being of the business, getting new business, keeping existing business, making money, making more money, making sure the government gets everything they need and above all making sure that our customers are happy and keep wanting to do business.

Most employees never see the wider scope of a boss's life and the juggling that goes on. That is why our actions often appear counter to their ideas of consistency and what makes sense. There is no way that they can know everything that the boss does but that does not prevent them from making judgments about the owner's actions based on their limited scope.

I can't tell you how many times I have heard how dumb the owners are or how much better that employee could run the business if they were as lucky as the boss to be in their position. In almost all cases luck as nothing to do with it. The people who are bosses and owners are there because they have earned it. They work harder, are smarter and are willing to take more chances and risk what they have to follow their dreams. There are very few stupid owners because in our capitalistic economy they will be eaten alive. However, there are lots of people who are jealous of their efforts and success and don't have the guts to try running things themselves.

I can change the world because:

Chapter 67

Even if you don't have the "title", we are all still salesmen.

Daniel

7/2/2000

I was sitting in Temple the other night and marveling at Daniel. He is the head Rabbi of our Temple, he is 35 years old, good looking, congenial, sweet and one of my two best friends. As I watched him begin and lead the service I was awestruck by his ability to move the congregation. His mixture of humility, humor, knowledge and his knack for being able to mold the individuals who came into the service into a single group of people is a joy to witness. He led that group of people through a mixture of emotional states that he had preplanned, to achieve the results of spiritual newness, calmness contentment and enjoyment. This ability of course resulted in more and more people coming to hear him preach which is what he wanted.

Daniel is a salesman and a great one. He recognizes the needs of his customers (his congregates) and prepares them spiritually and emotionally to handle what they need before he delivers it. He understands the idea that he cannot get what he wants from them until they get what they want first. He gives them spiritual renewal and a place of warmth and comfort where they can go without question and they in turn pay their membership fees, go to various productions and support him in his bid for pay raises, more help and anything else that he wants.

He is in a contract, just like all other "salesman" and realizes he has to deliver first before he can get what he wants. In my opinion only 5% of the world understands this idea, that to "get" you have to give first. It sounds like some hoaky religious ideal that you need to have patience, wait and serve others before you can get what you want. But the truth is that it is the only way to get the success in the levels to which you seek and if you don't go from that perspective then you are destined for a life of increasingly depleting returns on your time and energy.

My first rule of selling is that you can never sell anyone anything unless you find out what they want and satisfy that need first. This rule applies to life in all areas and the sooner it's power is understood then the faster you can get what you want.

I know a man who is self-motivated. By that I mean he judges the world first through his own eyes and then others. He is pleasant, bright, quick and loyal but he is not outward thinking person. He lives his life from the self-side and is therefore constantly in trouble with his co-workers and boss. He is constantly embroiled in minor hassles because he cannot look from the outside first. People do not trust him because of his self-centeredness and he will never go as far as he might have because of his inability to see it from another's viewpoint. This does not mean he is not intelligent or doesn't have many positive characteristics, it simply means that he lacks this ability to be empathetic and this, like most others in this world will make his road to his goals much longer and rockier.

You then may ask that if you cannot innately be able to see what others see, then are you destined to not reach your goals and have a much tougher time in life? The answer is no. This type of cognitive thinking, of being able to see from the other side is a learnable skill and with practice can surpass those who have it naturally.

Why? Because if it is innate, then you then it will probably be selective to certain areas of life which is also self limiting. If you have to learn it, you can go across all of the strata of your life through all experiences and relationships and achieve a much broader advantage from the ability. Think of it as the big leagues in baseball. The best home run hitters are often "naturals" and don't know why they hit the ball the way they do. The best coaches are the ones who started with little or no talent and through drive and determination structured their lives so that they could concentrate on utilizing and maximizing the small amount of talent they had.

The same is true here, I was not a natural at anything and therefore had to learn everything from scratch. With the basics that my father had given me, I learned, over time, and I am still learning, to be able to watch people, try to understand what makes them tick, and from there, formulate a system for understanding why they act as they do.

Many people are driven by emotion, they do not know why they do things. In essence there are a few reasons why people react as they do, most of it stems from primal instincts. People like to own things, it is theirs and no one can take it away. People also like to have others do what they say and like to be thought of as "in charge." People also like to be thought of as smart, and to be respected.

In truth, do most people deserve to be rich, and treated like saints? The answer is no. But that has nothing to do with their perception of life and their place in it. If they are not being treated as they think they deserve then they are probably frustrated and unhappy to some degree. If you are trying to sell them something you need to know about this before you can begin.

If you can understand where they are coming from then it will give you the blueprint as to how to act, to supply what they need so you can get, on a percentage basis what you want.

Again, since everything is from the outside, if you can posses the talent to understand what is happening inside the heads of your clients then you can partially control the situations you are in. You can start to maneuver and manipulate events to go to the areas that you want. Does it work every time? Of course not. Does it work on a percentage basis? Positively. How do you know what the percentage is? That depends on how good you are.

For now, try looking from the outside with a couple of people. One person you know, one person you know a little and a stranger. Talk to them, feel them out, within a few seconds of talking with them you can usually tell a lot of basic fundamentals about their personality. Are they outgoing or tight lipped, happy or sad, nice or mean, smart or not, of course they will fall in the middle of all of the grids. From that information you can formulate an idea of where they will stand on things and find out what they want in certain areas. For this test pick any subject like sports, work or politics.

Then you can pick a topic where you think they will have an opinion and have a conversation promoting their point of view. If you find them agreeing then you have read them correctly, and if it is different then you know you have misread them. What is the point?

In order to be able to get what you want you need to know what they want first. If you are trying to promote your new company and you find out that the "buyer" was in your same position five years ago and had gone bankrupt, your presentation will be markedly different that if the buyer was fresh out of college with no experience. You have to define your playing field, what the people want and fill that need before you get what you desire.

You have to think all of the time and can never let your "guard" down and be selfish or stop your outside feelers from picking up information. It is exhausting, exhilarating and fun because it means you can increasingly predict what will happen based on the "clues" you are given. The more you can "read" a situation, the more control you will have, and the greater your chances to give the other person what they want. You can then achieve your desired results.

NOTES

Chapter 68

Diamonds to you, rocks to me. Gourmet food to you, calories to me. Satisfaction for you, continual hunger for me.

$33.00 for Lobster

7/14/2002

In the early days of our country in Massachusetts, one of the stipulations often put into a servant's contract was that they could not be served lobster more than a specified number of times per week. Lobster was considered almost a garbage food and the workers did not want to have to eat it too often.

Hundreds of years later those contracts would probably read more like, you will be lucky if you get lobster more than once per year. What was garbage to one person was a delicacy to another, oh how a few hundred years can change a point of view. How often do we see the value of things change, almost before our eyes because of the way other people view them. Imagine $33.00 for a lobster dinner, our ancestors would never have believed it.

We do a great deal of work for the telecommunications industry and their collective fortunes have plummeted over the last few years. Most of our customers are down from 50-85% and many are just trying to survive. I see their struggle on a daily basis trying to hold unto what little business they have in the hope that the pipeline for ordering will be opened soon.

Fortunately or not, it is times like these where you have to look outward and into the future if you expect to be able to ride into the next business upswing. My grandfather started our company in 1921 and we have seen the roller coaster of business climates go from sky high to the basement and back again a bunch of times and some things do not change.

I have been after a piece of business for three years. One of our biggest customers created a unit constructed of metal parts that, although not revolutionary, could potentially have a profitable small market. That niche area is the problem because three years ago when all the Telecoms were very "hot" this project did not have the capability of hundred of millions of dollars in sales a year and was therefore not worth the time of my customer to develop and market it.

Our company, Ideal Jacobs had made some of the metal parts for the original prototype which is how we got involved and as I saw the project take shape I could see its potential, a few million dollars in sales a year is nothing to a multinational corporation but is a nice chunk of business for me. My customer put the project on indefinite hold.

Consequently I have spent the last two years trying to get control of the unit so my company can finish the development and then manufacture and market it. Here lies the problem, since the Telecoms have cooled off they now do not have money or manpower for a project like this. Had I not showed such an interest, I believe the project would have been scrapped instead of mothballed, our customer keeps re-evaluating it to see if they want to reactivate it.

For over two years they have been sitting on it, unwilling to give it up to me and accept royalties but unable to make a decision to move on it themselves. If I did not have faith in it then they would not either, it is like the lobster, they did not think it is good enough to do anything with it, but since I valued it highly, and they respect my opinion, they don't want to let it go for fear it will be bigger than they thought. It is a highly frustrating situation, I can see the potential and the money, the people who have control say they can also but won't make a move.

To add to the problem I believe they have decided that the finished product should sell for a specified price and make a minimum profit. That was back in the days of the boom when they had a massive sales force, plenty of support and little price pressure from their customers. It is just like the lobster, they think dinner should cost $80.00 but in today's marketplace it can only be sold for $33.00.

I am trying again; my newest proposal was submitted this morning. I am hoping that the combination of getting at least something for their efforts via royalties plus throwing in the benefit of getting me off their backs, a not inconsequential bonus, might be enough to swing them this time. Hopefully they will let me fly to their headquarters, get all the players into a closed room and we can try and settle this thing. I have no idea anymore, but in today's environment, or any time when I see a place for profit, I attack until I am either told to go away or get a piece or all of it.

Value is a purely subjective thing until someone you respect or fear has a different opinion of it than you. While I care nothing for lobster the lesson is universal, don't be ready to proclaim something useless if someone close to you thinks it has merit.

Sanctuary

7/16/2002

When I was growing up, I used to love going into my parents bedroom in the summer.

It would be hot outside but their air conditioner would be running, a baseball game would be on and my Dad would be lying on his bed asleep or close to it.

The feeling of hitting that blast of cold air and seeing the game on TV somehow gave me a feeling of walking into a sanctuary filled with peace, tranquility and knowing that all was well.

As I got older I learned to love the feeling I got when I had wrung everything good out of a day, utilizing every ounce of strength I had, mental, physical and emotional to maximize the best I could be. Therefore I would try to spend my days attacking in every area trying for the best in all and not missing anything. My wife would know by the way I was walking when I got home for dinner what type a day it had been and the wearier I looked the more she knew the hotter my bath would be.

My Dad's sanctuary was watching the ball game and mine is in a bathtub of incredibly hot water where I could escape for a little while everyday, reading and thinking about life.

I will leave you with this question. Do you have a place like my Dad and I where you can go to escape life for a little bit everyday? A place that is safe, warm and always there for you regardless of what else happens? A sanctuary that is yours alone?

If not, you might want to consider it. No matter how well you sell, how much money you make and how successful you are, you will need some time to get your head back together, if nothing else so you can recharge for what is coming tomorrow. Living your life to your limits can be a great deal of fun, but you might not realize it if you never give yourself the chance to stop and actually see what is going on. By the way, it is really okay to think about what a great job you did and take credit for your successes. It is also okay not to dwell too much on the stuff that went wrong, except to gain experience that will help you later.

Thanks for reading my book, if you have any questions, comments or want my opinion on anything please feel free to e-mail me at ***acj@idealjacobs.com***, or call me toll free at ***1-800-USE-IDEAL***.

GO SELL!

Colophon

This book was prepared using Adobe InDesign version 2.0.1 on a Pentium IV machine running WindowsXP Pro. The original text was supplied from the author as individual MSWord files. Style sheets and rough text formatting were applied in Word97 and WordXP to prepare the files for import into InDesign. Layout, setup, and print prep were performed by David W Creighton.

The body text is set in 10 point Myriad Roman, with chapter introductions set in 9 point Myriad Italic. The chapter headings are 14 point ITC New Baskerville Bold Italic, and the article titles are 14 point Myriad Bold. All fonts used in the document are PostScript Type 1 fonts.

The front and back covers were designed and illustrated by Michael Valentine using Adobe Illustrator version 10.0.1 on a G4 Macintosh running OS 9.2. The typefaces used on the covers are Present and AvantGarde.

The portrait of the author on the back cover was photographed by Marc Appezzato using a Nikon CoolPix 990 digital camera. The resulting 1672 x 1401 pixel image was cropped and corrected using Adobe Photoshop 6.0. The resulting 976 x 780 pixel image was scaled to 300dpi and embedded into the Adobe Illustrator cover file.

All type on the covers was converted to outlines before the files were saved in EPS format for import into InDesign. Bullets and checkboxes in the text were recreated as graphics in Illustrator to solve an outputting problem occuring with the print facility's RIP.

The finished layout was converted to a PDF (1.4) document using Adobe Acrobat Distiller. The resulting PDF file was used to transfer the volume to the print facility for imposition, setup, and printing.

DWC

NOTES